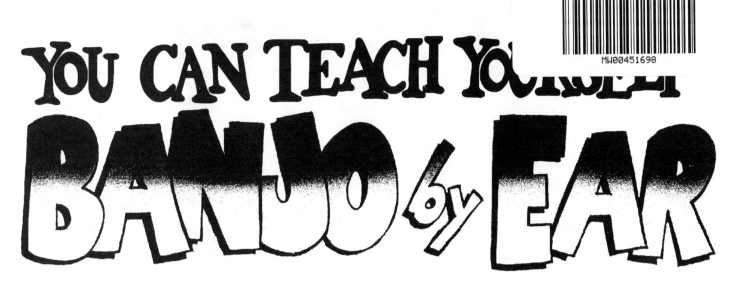

YOU CAN TEACH YOURSELF BANJO by EAR

by Jack Hatfield

INTRODUCTION

Learning to play a musical instrument is one of the most rewarding and satisfying experiences a music lover can have. As any endeavor that is worthwhile, though, it requires a lot of dedication and hard work.

It is very difficult to learn to play a musical instrument without the aid of a teacher or an instruction manual. There are many fine instruction manuals that are designed to make the learning process as efficient as possible via the printed page. Most teachers use these instruction manuals or write their own arrangements for students. Some students prefer to learn with the aid of self-instruction manuals or self-instructing video courses. These video instruction courses usually include tablature books to clarify and inform when a video player is not handy. Again, much of the information is conveyed via the printed page.

Though musical notation and tablature are incredibly important tools, they have their pitfalls. Often the student gets so comfortable with the routine of learning from the printed page that he or she never makes a conscious effort to develop listening skills. All the student can do is play by rote. In other words, the songs are played from memory exactly the same way each time, with no variation or improvisation.

Many musicians, even some that are technically advanced, never break away from the printed music and start teaching themselves to play by simply listening and re-creating. The common name for this process is "playing by ear". To those who have never tried, playing by ear seems like a vast and mysterious no-man's land. Many musicians either lack the necessary confidence or do not believe they are ready to learn by ear. The truth is that any musician with rudimentary skills can teach himself to play by ear if he is aware of some basic guidelines. That is what this book is all about.

It may seem contradictory that a book could teach you to play by ear. The fact is, the tools you need are largely conceptual. There are certain rules and probabilities that govern musical composition. There are also some basic building blocks that songs are composed of. If you are aware of these concepts and conventions, you will become incredibly more adept at playing by ear.

Along with the information, you need two other things: desire and experience. You undoubtedly have the desire or you would not have spent your hard-earned money on this book. You now have access to the information, so grab your banjo and let's get some experience.

CD CONTENTS

Visit us on the Web at http://www.melbay.com — E-mail us at email@melbay.com

1 2 3 4 5 6 7 8 9 0

Jack Hatfield

ABOUT THE AUTHOR

   Jack Hatfield has been a professional instructor of banjo for over 20 years at the time of this printing. He has taught thousands to play the banjo via his instruction book series entitled *Bluegrass Banjo Method.* He has been a regular monthly contributor to *Banjo Newsletter* magazine for 15 years. *Banjo Newsletter* is the foremost source of banjo information in the world. His Scruggs Corner columns analyzed the work of Earl Scruggs, the "father of bluegrass banjo". These transcriptions remain today the most complete and accurate body of Earl's recordings ever published. Jack then wrote the Beginner's Corner column for 6 years, in which he tutored novice banjoists. He is currently writing a column called Concepts and Systems, in which he explains the structure of music as applied to the five-string banjo and reveals procedures and systems of learning that give the student a conceptual view of the music. He has also published songbooks for banjo, fiddle, mandolin and guitar with coinciding play-along rhythm tapes, and published a unique book for all musicians called *How to Play by Ear — A Guide to Chords and Progressions for Musicians, Songwriters, and Composers.*

   Jack is band leader/banjoist for the *True Blue* bluegrass band, which works conventions and tourist attractions such as *Dollywood* theme park and the *Dixie Stampede* in his home town of Pigeon Forge, Tennessee. He has been a finalist in the Tennessee State Banjo Championship, the Kentucky State Banjo Championship, and the National Banjo Championship held in Winfield, Kansas.

HOW TO READ TABLATURE

Tablature is a method of writing music for stringed instruments that shows what notes to play graphically instead of by standard musical notation. Here is how it works:

Banjo tablature has five lines. Each line represents one of the banjo strings. The first (top) line represents the first (bottom) string of the banjo. The second line represents the second (from the bottom) string, and so on.

A number on one of the lines indicates at what fret to note that string.

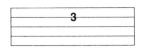

Play the second string, third fret

A zero means to play the corresponding string open.

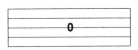

Play the third string, open.

The letter under the note indicates which right hand finger to use.

T = Thumb, I = Index,
M = Middle, P = Pinch

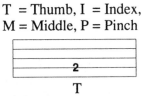

4th. string, 2nd fret, use R. <u>Thumb</u>

A *beat* is a unit of time. All beats are equidistant in time unless noted by the composer. Beats are grouped into equal divisions called *measures* or *bars.* These are sectioned off by the use of vertical *measure lines* or *bar lines,* which make it easier to count time and keep your place. The *time signature,* which appears at the beginning of the tune in standard musical notation, can alter the number of beats per measure or the time allowed to the various note types. Almost all banjo tablature is written in 4/4 time, meaning there are four beats in each measure and a quarter note receives one beat. The time signature is usually not used in banjo tablature unless the piece is in 3/4 time, in which there are three beats in each measure and a quarter note receives one beat.

Duration is indicated by the use of *stems, beams,* and *flags.* A *stem* is a vertical line attached to a note. A *beam* is a heavy horizontal line connecting two or more notes. A *flag* is a pennant-shaped mark attached to a stem. A note that stands alone with a stem is a *quarter note.* It lasts one full beat. A note that either has a single flag and stands alone or is attached to another note or notes by a single beam is an *eighth note.* It lasts one-half a beat. A note that either has two flags and stands alone or is attached to other notes by two beams is a *sixteenth note.* It lasts one fourth of a beat.

Repeat marks consist of two vertical lines with a colon next to them, and indicate that a part of the song is to be played again. A large "squiggle" mark is a *quarter rest.* It denotes one beat of silence. A heavy dash attached to the third line is a *half rest.* It denotes two beats of silence. A *tie* is a curved line that connects two notes. It signifies that the first note is to be played and held the duration of both notes added together. For example, two quarter notes joined by a tie signify a single note that lasts two beats. The *chords* will be shown in bold type above the tablature. This is primarily for the rhythm players, but can give the lead player valuable hints about left-hand fingering. *Melody notes* will be in boldface type. *Fill notes* will be in regular type. *Hammer-ons, pull-offs* and *slides* will be shown by a dash between two notes and the letter *h, p* or *s* underneath. A sample tablature appears below with features labeled.

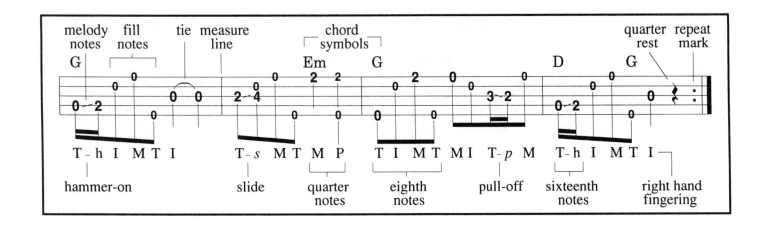

TABLE OF CONTENTS

Chapter 1

LEARNING CHORD PROGRESSIONS BY EAR

The banjo is a very chord-oriented instrument. Unlike most instruments, the banjo makes use of chords both in accompaniment *and* in lead playing. For this reason, it is extremely important for the banjoist who wishes to learn songs by ear to be able to first identify the component chords. The banjoist can "fake" a song by ear (play an approximation of the melody) after very little study time if he knows the chord progression. As he gains familiarity with the song, a more accurate and complete melody arrangement can be devised, based on the faked solo.

The first goal of this book will be to teach you some basics about chord progressions in order to streamline the trial-and-error procedure that is used to identify the chords to a song. With this in mind, let us now examine how chords relate to other components of music.

Elements of Music

The most basic element of music is the *note*. A note is a specific frequency of sound waves which is experienced by the human ear as a musical pitch. There are 12 notes in our system of music, each separated by an interval of a *half-step* (a one-fret interval) or a *whole-step* (a two-fret interval). Using various arrangements of half-step and whole-step intervals, different *scales* can be constructed. The most commonly used scales are the *major scale* and the (melodic) *minor scale*. The *melody* is a pleasing arrangement of notes, generally selected from the scale, and played in sequence. *Chords* are formed by selecting three or four notes from the scale and playing them simultaneously. The notes in a chord can also be played in sequence, which is called an *arpeggio*. Scruggs-style banjo playing can be thought of as a continuous arpeggio. The chords are arranged by the composer to provide harmony for the melody line. The scale, its inherent chords, and the relationships therein form a motif called a *key*. Add to these components the organizing aspect of *rhythm,* and you have *music.*

Counting Time and Determining the Location of Chord Changes

The most basic element of rhythm is the *beat.* A beat is a steady pulse. A heartbeat or the ticking of a clock are good examples. Unless otherwise instructed by the composer, all beats within a composition are equidistant in time. Individual beats are grouped into larger units of equal length. Each one of these units is called a *measure,* or *bar.* These measures are grouped into still larger segments called *song parts.* In an instrumental tune, these song parts are often referred to as the *A part, B part, C part,* etc. In a vocal number, there are typically two song parts. A song part that appears two or more times with the same melody line and chord progression and non-repeating lyrics is called a *verse.* A song part that appears two or more times with a repeating melody line, chord progression, and lyrics is called a *chorus.* The verse and chorus can have the same melody line and chord structure, but the repetition or non-repetition of the lyrics can define them as different song parts. The verse is usually sung by a solo vocalist. The chorus usually employs vocal harmony. There are some songs, particularly ballads, that have no chorus — they are composed entirely of verses. Some songs contain a third part which only appears once and has a melody and chord progression that is different from the verse and chorus. This song part is called a *bridge.* The bridge almost always appears before the last chorus. The bridge part is rare in folk, old-time and bluegrass music styles, but if you will be learning country or popular songs by ear, you should be aware of it.

Most vocal numbers also contain *solos,* or "breaks", as they are frequently called. A solo consists of a musician playing a song part instrumentally. The instrumentalist sometimes plays an abbreviated solo that has a special function in the song. This mini-solo can come in the form of an *intro, turnaround,* or *ending.* Though abbreviated intros are seldom employed in music styles that include the five-string banjo, many songs begin with a full instrumental solo. Turnarounds are occasionally used to start a song (especially in gospel music), and endings are almost always present.

The number of beats assigned to each measure is one of the factors that determines the *meter* of a composition. Most music styles that commonly include the banjo use one of only four meters: 2/4 time (also called "march time"), 4/4 time (also called "common time"), 3/4 time (also called "waltz time") and 6/8 time (sometimes called "jig time"). For our purposes, any of these meters can be interpreted in 4/4 time or 3/4 time.

7

The first beat of each measure is normally accented (played slightly louder than the other beats), creating a pulse that is easily identified. Important chord changes generally take place on the first beat of a measure. If there is another chord change within the measure, it usually occurs on the third beat.

Note that the first word of the lyrics and/or the first note played by an instrumentalist is seldom the first beat of a measure. Most songs have *pickup notes* that are of less than a full measure in length. Usually these pickup notes are played or sung by a soloist, and the full band starts playing on the first beat of the first *complete* measure. That is where the chord progression actually starts.

To determine which meter to interpret a song in, simply listen for the first chord to be played by the rhythm instruments, and start counting either "**One** two, three, four, **One** two three four..." or "**One**, two three, **One**, two three...", stressing the count of "**One**". It should be immediately apparent if you are counting in the wrong meter — the chord changes and the beginning of the vocal or instrumental phrases will seem "out of synch" with your count.

Exercise 1

DETERMINING METER

On the recording that accompanies this book, the melody is on the left channel and the rhythm instruments are on the right. Turn the balance control of your stereo fully to the right so the melody will not tip you off as to the name of the song. Listen to the progressions of song examples #1–#12. Each example will be played in either 3/4 time or in 4/4 time. Determine the meter and circle the correct answer below. *The answers can be found on page 93.*

1 3/4 4/4	4 3/4 4/4	7 3/4 4/4	10 3/4 4/4
2 3/4 4/4	5 3/4 4/4	8 3/4 4/4	11 3/4 4/4
3 3/4 4/4	6 3/4 4/4	9 3/4 4/4	12 3/4 4/4

Locating Chord Changes

We will now try to determine where the chord changes occur in a song. Listen to the sample song on the recording. Concentrate only on the rhythm instruments, particularly the bass. The various instruments combine to form a matrix of sound with a basic tone that can be identified as the *root* of the chord. We are not going to try to identify the chord right now — we are only concerned with where in the song the chords change.

Exercise 2

LOCATING SIMPLE CHORD CHANGES

With the balance control of your stereo turned fully to the right, listen carefully to the progressions of Song Examples #1–#3 on the recording. In the blank chord charts that follow, each box represents one measure. Note the meter (3/4 time or 4/4 time) in the space provided. Above the diagram, mark a small "x" after the measure line where each chord change occurs. Do not be concerned with the name of the chord now, merely at what point it changes. The sample progression is worked for you. *The answers can be found on page 93.*

Verse/Chorus:

Sample Progression
Meter:_____4/4_____

Verse/Chorus:

Progression #1:
Meter:_____

Verse:

Progression #2:
Meter:_____

Chorus:

9

Progression #3:
Meter:_____

Exercise 3

HEARING CHORD CHANGES WITHIN THE MEASURE

With the balance control of your stereo turned fully to the right, listen to the progressions of Song Examples #4–#6. In these examples, the chords may change not only on the first beat of the measure, but also within the measure. Each box is subdivided into the proper number of segments to correspond with the meter. Mark a small "x" above the part of the box that corresponds with the location of each chord change. *The answers appear on page 94.*

Progression #4:
Meter:_____4/4_____

Verse:

Chorus:

Progression #5:
Meter:_____4/4_____

Verse:

Chorus:

Progression #6:
Meter:_____3/4_____

Verse/Chorus:

Simplifying the Trial-and-Error Procedure

Figuring out a chord progression is largely a trial-and-error procedure — there is simply no substitute for experimentation. It can be compared to learning to drive a car: You can read the driver's manual and become knowledgeable about traffic laws and driving techniques. You can come to understand the car's mechanics and the theory behind the internal combustion engine. But you cannot learn to drive a car until you get behind the wheel and become part of the driving experience.

Until you take part in the trial-and-error procedure of listening, guessing a note or a chord, and playing that note or chord on your instrument to check out the accuracy of your guess, you will never learn to play by ear. This book is not a magic wand that will make you into an instant "ear" player — nothing can do that.

This book is, however, an aid that will teach you basic fundamentals about keys and chord progressions so that the trial-and-error procedure can be simplified immensely. It will also catalogue some basic licks that you can use as building blocks, giving you a "vocabulary" of licks that you can use to construct arrangements to literally thousands of songs. If you are at the intermediate skill level or above, you probably play most of these licks already. You may not, however, view them as licks — phrases that can be played independently at will and arranged in different combinations to create specific melodies. If you are a beginner with only fundamental skills, you will learn these licks later in this book. Before we begin the actual work of learning to play by ear, however, let us first learn some basics about chords.

The Diatonic Triads

We will work exclusively in the key of G, since the popular three-finger bluegrass banjo style is generally played on a G-tuned instrument, and most banjoists think in the key of G. There are seven basic three-note chords that are generated from the seven degrees of the G major scale. They are called the *diatonic triads*. They are as follows:

The Diatonic Triads						
G	Am	Bm	C	D	Em	F♯°
1	2	3	4	5	6	7

The Three Basic Chords

Some of these chords are used more frequently than others. The chords that are based on the 1, 4 and 5 degrees of the major scale are by far the most popular. It is estimated that over 75 percent of all bluegrass, folk, gospel, and old-time country songs are composed of only these three chords. In the key of G, these are the G, C and D chords. Since most banjoists are more familiar with the key of G, all examples in this book will be in that key. If you wish to study a song in another key, refer to the transposition chart on page 118. Let us now examine the function of the three basic chords in order to gain insights that will help us recognize them more easily when we hear them in a song.

The G chord (the 1 chord) functions as the "home base" of the chord progression. The G chord is called the *tonic*. As you play the chords to a song, think of yourself as a traveler on a round-trip journey. The G chord is usually the starting point, and practically always the final destination, of a song part or a phrase. The other chords in the progression can be considered as either interesting stops along the way or alternate routes.

Since the G chord holds this important position, it is naturally the most frequently occurring chord in the progression. When you arrive at the G chord "destination", it is often like a period at the end of a sentence. There is a sense of finality, or a sense of an idea being completed. If you listen to the lyrics and the chord progression with this in mind, you can probably pick out many of the G chords in a song.

The D chord (the 5 chord) is known as the *dominant* chord. It is the next most frequently visited destination of our musical "traveler". You could think of the D chord as having the strongest "pull", drawing the traveler away from the G chord. The most basic progression consists of just the G chord and the D chord. There are actually one-chord songs, such as *Three Blind Mice, Frere Jaque,* and other children's songs, but they hardly qualify as progressions. Some well-known examples of G–D songs are *Tom Dooley, Oh, My Darling, Clementine,* and *Train '45*. It should be noted that the D chord is often voiced as a D7, especially when it occurs just before the final G chord in a song part.

The C chord (the 4 chord) is the next most frequently used chord. It is known as the *subdominant*. It appears almost as frequently as the D chord, typically in songs that are comprised of three chords or more. It rarely appears as the "other chord" in a two-chord progression. This can be a valuable clue in itself. If you are trying to figure out a song that has three distinct chord sounds in it, and you can identify the G and D chords, it is extremely likely that the mystery chord is the C chord. Another clue — on the occasion that a song part does not start on the G chord, it usually starts on the C chord.

Listening for Repetition

Most melody lines and chord progressions involve some repetition. If a melody line is repeated, then the chances are extremely good that the accompanying chord progression is being repeated. This can save a great deal of work when figuring out progressions. Before beginning to learn a chord progression by ear, listen to the song a few times. Focus on the melody if it is an instrumental tune. If it is a vocal song, focus on the melody and the lyrics. The repetition of lyrics can be an obvious clue — every time you hear a given lyrical phrase, the chords that accompany it will usually be the same. If the lyrics *and* the accompanying melody line repeat, it is virtually a certainty that the coinciding chords repeat also.

There are many songs in which the progression of the entire verse and chorus are identical. In these cases, figuring out the first song part gives you the chords to the entire song. Progression #1, Progression #3, and Progression #6 are examples of this. With the balance control of your stereo adjusted to the middle position, listen to these examples, noting the repetition of melody and chord structure.

Repetition of phrases within the song part is also very common. In 4/4 time, song parts are usually eight measures in length. The component phrases are generally two or four measures long. Progression #5 illustrates this. Listen to the example on the recording, following along on the diagram on the next page. You will notice in the verse that there is an almost exact repetition of melody every two measures. Measures one and two could be called Phrase A. Measures three and four repeat, but not exactly. We will call them Phrase B. Measures five and six are an exact repetition of Phrase A. Measures seven and eight are an almost exact repetition of Phrase A. We will designate them Phrase C, since they are not duplicates of Phrase A:

	Phrase A		Phrase B		Phrase A		Phrase C	
Progression #5 Verse:	G	G C	G	G D	G	G C	G	D G

If you recognize the repetition in the verse of Progression #5, you will reduce the amount of work required to figure out the chord progression by a fourth. This 8-measure verse is composed of only three 2-measure phrases — we have reduced the amount of work from 8 measures to 6.

Return to the recording and listen to the chorus part of Progression #5. It can be broken down into two 4-measure phrases, which we will call Phrase D. By recognizing repetition, the work of deducing the chords has been reduced by half:

	Phrase D				Phrase D			
Progression #5 Chorus:	G			D G	G			D G

When listening to a band and trying to identify chords by ear, the single most important instrumental voice to notice is the bass. The bass player usually plays the root note of the chord on the first beat of the measure, and on the first beat of any new chord, no matter where in the measure the new chord appears. In 3/4 time, the bassist usually plays the root note on the first beat of the measure and holds it through the second and third beats. If the chord lasts more than one measure, he will either play the root note on every first beat or alternate the root and 5 note every other first beat until a new chord appears.

In so doing, the bass player defines the basic chord being played at any given time. The chord type (major, minor, seventh, etc.) cannot be discerned by listening to the bass player alone, because it takes at least three notes to fully define a chord. But in order to identify a chord, you must first identify the root note. Therefore, the note played by the bass player on the first beat of the measure is the best clue as to the letter name of the chord.

Exercise 4

LEARNING "BASIC THREE" PROGRESSIONS BY EAR

With the balance control of your stereo adjusted to the middle position, listen again to progressions of Song Examples #1–#6, for which you have already determined the meter and location of the chord changes. By listening for repetition, using the process of elimination, and listening to the bass player, determine the identity of the chords by ear.

First listen to the entire progression to identify any repetition of melody line and/or lyrics. If you do detect repetition, you may want to mark the phrases on the blank chord chart in advance. If you are not sure, mark the chord chart anyway, and check out the possibility of repetition as you progress.

Start the recording, stopping it immediately after you hear the first chord. You must learn to listen to the unknown chord and remember its sound until you can check its identity with your banjo. It will be very difficult to concentrate on the chord in question if the recording is allowed to proceed to the next chord.

Guess the identity of the first chord, using the process of elimination. In other words, guess G chord first. Play a G chord on your instrument. Listen to see if it matches the sound on the recording, paying special attention to the bass note. If it does not sound like a G chord, try the next most likely choice, the D chord. If the G and D chords are eliminated, the "mystery chord" is almost certainly the C chord.

As you identify each chord, fill in the blank chord chart (pages 9 and 10) and proceed to the next chord. Remember, there are only three basic chords. Therefore, once you have identified a chord, you only have two possible choices for the following chord — if the chord changes, the new chord cannot possibly be the same one just played.

Remember, also — most song parts start on the 1 chord (the G chord in these examples) and almost always end on the 1 chord. If the song part does not start on the G chord, the C chord is the next most probable.

After you have identified the first couple of changes, listen again for repetition of phrases. *The answers can be found on pages 94–95.*

The Supporting Chords

The chords that appear in the 2, 3, and 6 positions of the diatonic chord scale can be thought of as the *diatonic supporting chords,* much like the supporting actors in a play or a movie. In the key of G, these are the A, B, and E chords. In formal music, these chords can be voiced as minor triads or they can be voiced as seventh chords. However, in banjo-related styles such as bluegrass, folk, and old-time country, they are often voiced as the "theoretically incorrect" major types.

The flatted 7 major chord and the flatted 3 major chord can be considered the *modal supporting chords.* These are the F major chord and the B flat major chord in the key of G. They are generated not from the G scale, but by a particular *mode* of that scale. A mode is like an offshoot major scale built on each step of the key scale. The modal chords lend a bluesy or melancholy feel, making them fairly easy to discern.

The 7 chord (the F sharp diminished chord in the key of G) is rarely used in traditional music, so we can eliminate it from our palette to make the guesswork somewhat easier.

Functions of the Supporting Chords

The supporting chords do not appear as often as do the "basic three". When they do appear, they can serve one or more of three functions: *a)* to embellish the chord progression, giving it more interest, *b)* as a functional *substitute* for one of the basic three chords, or *c)* to act as a *transition* or stepping stone from one chord to another.

Embellishment

Supporting chords can be inserted between basic chord changes or in place of the basic chords merely to "spice up" an otherwise simple or predictable progression. The 6m and the 3m chords are often used in place of the 1 chord for this purpose. In the key of G, these are the Em and Bm chords, respectively. The G chord in measure 13 of *Amazing Grace* below was changed to an Em chord to demonstrate this principle. The Em chord harmonizes the melody nicely and provides some harmonic interest to an otherwise predictable progression:

Amazing Grace — Basic Progression

G   G   C   G   G   G   D   D   G   G   C   G   G   D   G   G

Amazing Grace — Em Chord Substituting for G Chord as Embellishment

G   G   C   G   G   G   D   D   G   G   C   G   Em   D   G   G

Sometimes the supporting chords are played in sequence based on ascending or descending scale movement. This can be done within the song, or can serve as an ending as in the example below. Again using *Amazing Grace* to demonstrate, we replace the last two measures of the G chord with a descending chord scale segment that changes on each beat, "walking" down the scale from the C chord to the final G chord. *Note* — The chords in parentheses are all within the same measure, one chord played on each beat.

Amazing Grace — Chord Scale Embellishment Ending

G G C G   G G D D   G G C G   G D (C-Bm-Am) G

Major-type chords are sometimes voiced instead as seventh types to lend a bluesy or jazzy atmosphere or to create a feeling of tension. This is often done with blues progressions. Contrast the difference in the standard twelve-bar blues progression below played with all major chords to the same progression using all seventh chords:

Twelve-Bar Blues — All Major Chords

G G G G   C C G G   D D G G

Twelve-Bar Blues — All Seventh Chords

G7 G7 G7 G7   C7 C7 G7 G7   D7 D7 G7 G7

Substitutions

Note that the "basic three" chords do not all have to be present in order for one or more of the supporting chords to be used. A progression can contain only three chords and still include a supporting chord. When this occurs, the supporting chord can be viewed as a functional substitute for one of the "basic three" chords. Often in bluegrass and old-time music the F chord is used as a substitute for the D chord. *Old Joe Clark* is an example. In the original old-time version, the verse and chorus were identical, containing only the G, C and D chords. At some point the F chord was inserted to substitute for one of the D chords in the chorus. Both choices harmonize with the melody line, and the use of the F chord in the chorus adds interest. This version of *Old Joe Clark* became popular through the years and is now considered by most musicians the "correct" way to play the song.

Old Joe Clark

Verse:	G	G	G	D	G	G	G/D	G
	G	G	G	D	G	G	G/D	G
Chorus:	G	G	G	F	G	G	G/D	G
	G	G	G	F	G	G	G/D	G

The Em chord can be used as a substitute for the G chord or the C chord. Since it has two notes in common with both chords, it harmonizes many of the same melody situations.

We demonstrated the use of the Em as a substitute for the G chord with the song *Amazing Grace* earlier in this chapter. To show how the Em can serve as a functional substitute for the C chord, consider the progression of *Lonesome Road Blues* below:

Lonesome Road Blues

G	G	G	G	C	C	G	G
C	C	G	G	D	D	G	G

Replace the C chords with Em chords, and you have *Foggy Mountain Breakdown:*

Foggy Mountain Breakdown

G	G	G	G	Em	Em	G	G
Em	Em	G	G	D	D	G	G

We can carry this idea a step further by studying the chord progression of *Bluegrass Breakdown.* In this three-part instrumental, the same kind of substitution is employed, using the F chord to function as a C chord in the first two parts.

Bluegrass Breakdown

A Part:	G	G	G	G	F	F	G	G
	F	F	G	G	D	D	G	G

B Part:	G	G	G	G	F	F	G	G
	F	F	G	G	D	D	G	G

C Part:	G	G	G	G	C	C	G	G
	C	C	G	G	D	D	G	G

Functionally, these three chord progressions are all the same. The role of the C chord is played by the Em chord in *Foggy Mountain Breakdown* and by the F chord in *Bluegrass Breakdown.* To demonstrate the concept of substitution further, you could actually "fake" a solo to one of these songs if you know a lead arrangement to one of the others: Simply play the right-hand part of one song, using the chord progression of the other.

These examples show that the only chord that is absolutely essential to the three-chord format is the key chord (the G chord in our examples). The C and the D chords can be substituted with supporting chords. If you realize this, many of the songs that contain supporting chords may make more sense to you. They may be functionally the same as "basic three" songs you already know, but a supporting chord may be doing the work of a "basic three" chord.

Listed below are common substitutions for the "basic three" chords in the key of G major. Remember, to qualify as a substitute, the chord must harmonize well with the melody line.

Substitutes for G: Em, Bm, (G7 especially when followed by a C chord)

Substitutes for C: F, Am, Em (C7 especially when followed by an F chord)

Substitutes for D: Am, F, Bm, (D7 especially when followed by a G chord)

Transitions

Another function of the supporting chords is to act as transitions or "stepping stones" between two other chords. For example, the chord change from G to D can be made more interesting and less abrupt if you insert the A chord before the D chord, as in measure six of *Amazing Grace* below. Listen and you will understand what is meant by "transition" — the A chord seems to "lead" the ear from the G chord to the D chord.

Amazing Grace — A Chord Serving as Transition

G G C G   G A D D   G G C G   G D G G

The A chord can also be voiced as an A7 chord for even greater effect. It contains certain internal dynamics that cause it to "pull" more strongly to the D chord.

Amazing Grace — A7 Chord Serving as Transition

G   G   C   G   G   A7   D   D   G   G   C   G   G   D   G   G

Using the Law of Probabilities

Among the chords discussed so far, we have discovered some clear-cut probabilities. You know that if you only hear three chords in a key-of-G song, they are probably the G, C and D chords. It was shown that of these basic three chords, the G chord is the most likely to occur. The D chord is next most likely, followed by the C chord. Knowing these probabilities helps you to eliminate a considerable amount of guesswork when trying to identify an unknown chord. Simply guess the most probable chord first. If it is incorrect, guess the next most probable chord, and so on.

If a song part in the key of G does not start on the G chord, it is extremely likely that it starts on the C chord. Therefore, if the chord is heard to change at the beginning of a song part (the previous part will virtually always end on the G chord), always try the C chord as your first guess.

Of the supporting chords, the A and E chords are most likely to appear, followed by the F chord. The B chord and the B-flat chord are much less likely. Remember, the A, E and B chords can be played as minor or seventh type chords, but in traditional music styles, these chords are frequently played as major types.

To condense the information presented so far, we can construct a probability chart based on how a chord functions within a progression. Here are the most-used chords in the key of G major, listed roughly in the order of occurrence:

Chord Function Probability Chart — Key of G Major

G, D, C, A (Am or A7), E (Em or E7), F, B (B7 or Bm), B-flat

Most-used chords   Least-used chords

Use the blank chord chart below to experiment with embellishments, substitutions, and transitions on a song you already play.

LEARNING PROGRESSIONS CONTAINING ONE SUPPORTING CHORD

Turn the balance control of your stereo fully to the right speaker to isolate the rhythm instruments. The progressions of Song Examples #7–#9 on the accompanying recording may contain any or all of the "basic three" chords plus one of the supporting chords, the A (Am or A7), E (Em or E7), F, B (B7 or Bm), or B-flat. Determine the location of the chord changes, then determine the name of each chord, using the probability chart on the previous page as a guide. Write the chord name in the appropriate box. If you are unsure about a chord, leave its box blank for now. We will learn some information in the next section that may help you figure it out. *The answers can be found on page 96.*

Progression #7:
Meter:_____4/4_____

Verse/Chorus:

Progression #8:
Meter:_____4/4_____

Verse/Chorus:

Progression #9:
Meter:_____4/4_____

Verse:

Chorus:

LEARNING PROGRESSIONS CONTAINING TWO SUPPORTING CHORDS

The progressions of Song Examples #10–#12 on the accompanying recording may contain any or all of the "basic three" chords plus two supporting chords, the A (Am or A7), E (Em or E7), F, B (B7 or Bm), or B-flat. Determine the location of the chord changes, then determine the name of each chord, using the probability chart on page 19 to guide your guesswork. Fill in the chord name in the appropriate box below. If you are unsure about a chord, leave the box blank for now. The next section contains information that may help you figure it out. *The answers an be found on pages 96–97.*

Verse/Chorus:

Progression #10:
Meter:_____4/4_____

Verse/Chorus:

Progression #11:
Meter:_____4/4_____

Verse/Chorus:

Progression #12:
Meter:_____4/4_____

Recognizing Chord Types

The next step in learning chord progressions by ear is to learn to identify the type of a given chord. By *type* we mean simply whether a chord is a major, a minor or seventh chord. Each of these chord types have their own unique qualities that are easily discerned. The various chord types serve only a few basic functions and show up in fairly predictable combinations within a chord progression. By simply knowing what these functions and combinations are, you can make the guesswork easier still. You can often deduce a chord's letter name if you can identify its type.

Emotional Characteristics

There are two primary qualities that chords possess. Being able to identify these qualities will help you determine the chord type. The first quality has to do with what kind of mood or emotion a chord evokes in the listener.

A major chord evokes a happy, bright or carefree mood. Play a G major chord and listen for the happy, bright quality that it evokes.

A minor chord evokes a sad, somber or serious mood. Play a Gm chord, comparing it to the G major chord just played. Can you hear the sad quality of the G minor?

A seventh chord evokes a tense or nervous feeling in the listener. Play a G7 chord, noting the nervous or irritating effect it evokes.

These qualities are true for any chord, regardless of its letter name. A G major does not sound any more or less bright and happy than a C major chord. It is the arrangement of intervals in the chord that produces the emotional characteristics. These emotional characteristics are fairly obvious once you know to listen for them. It is a short leap from being aware of a chord's emotional quality to identifying its type.

Use the blank chord chart below to record a progression or to experiment.

Consonance and Dissonance

The other quality that can be discerned in a chord is the degree of consonance or dissonance created by the component notes. A *consonant* harmony is a pleasant one. A *dissonant* harmony is an unpleasant or harsh one. Play a G note (third string; open). Now play a B note (second string; open). Play the G note and the B note simultaneously. The interval between the two notes is a *major third,* which is one of the more pleasant intervals.

MAJOR THIRD INTERVAL (CONSONANT)

Now play the same G note, but locate it on the fourth string; fifth fret. Play a B-flat note, which you will find on the third string; third fret. This interval is a *minor third.* It is perceived to be less dissonant than a major third, but is still tolerable to the ear.

MINOR THIRD INTERVAL (MILDLY DISSONANT)

Now play a B note (second string; open). Then play an F note (first string; third fret). Play the two notes simultaneously. This is a *tritone* interval (three whole-steps) which is one of the more unpleasant, or dissonant intervals.

TRITONE INTERVAL (VERY DISSONANT)

What was just demonstrated is three varying degrees of dissonance. The major third is the identifying interval of a major-type chord. Play a G major chord and identify the major third interval. The minor third is the identifying interval in a minor chord. Play a G minor chord and identify the two notes that create a minor third interval. The tritone is the identifying interval of a dominant seventh chord. Play a G7 chord and identify the two notes that create the tritone interval.

Listening for the degree of dissonance will help you determine whether a chord is of a major, minor or seventh type. Major chords have the most pleasant harmony. Minor chords are slightly less pleasant to the ear. Of the three types discussed, seventh chords have the most dissonant harmony — one that actually creates tension.

Of course there are other intervals in these chords. There are three notes in the major and minor chord, and four notes in the seventh chord. The distance between any two of these notes is an interval. A chord's type is defined by all of the component intervals. We have merely focused on the interval that is most responsible for the character of the major, minor and seventh chord to help illustrate consonance and dissonance.

If you listen for the emotional quality and the amount of consonance or dissonance within a chord, you should be able to determine whether any chord is a major, minor, or seventh type. Most people (even non-musicians) can identify major, minor and seventh chords by listening for the emotional aspect alone.

IDENTIFYING MAJOR, MINOR AND SEVENTH CHORD TYPES

Listen to the demonstration recording that accompanies this book. A chord will be played on the banjo. It may be any chord in the key of G. The letter name of the chord is not important. Listen for the emotional characteristics and the degree of consonance or dissonance and determine whether the chord is of the A) *major* B) *minor* or C) *seventh* type. Circle the correct answer. *The answers can be found on page 97.*

1	A	B	C		21	A	B	C
2	A	B	C		22	A	B	C
3	A	B	C		23	A	B	C
4	A	B	C		24	A	B	C
5	A	B	C		25	A	B	C
6	A	B	C		26	A	B	C
7	A	B	C		27	A	B	C
8	A	B	C		28	A	B	C
9	A	B	C		29	A	B	C
10	A	B	C		30	A	B	C
11	A	B	C		31	A	B	C
12	A	B	C		32	A	B	C
13	A	B	C		33	A	B	C
14	A	B	C		34	A	B	C
15	A	B	C		35	A	B	C
16	A	B	C		36	A	B	C
17	A	B	C		37	A	B	C
18	A	B	C		38	A	B	C
19	A	B	C		39	A	B	C
20	A	B	C		40	A	B	C

Movement in Fourths and the Dominant Seventh Chord

It was explained earlier that the "basic three" chords and the supporting chords serve distinct functions within a chord progression. The basic three (the G, C and D chords) are the framework of most progressions. The supporting chords (the A, B, and E-rooted chords and the F and B-flat major) chords, serve one or more of the following functions: *a)* embellishment, *b)* substitutes for one of the "basic three", or *c)* as transitions.

We are now going to explore the idea of transition further by learning about the dominant seventh chord type and a kind of chord progression logic that is completely different from "basic three" movement. The dominant seventh chord (commonly referred to as simply "seventh" chord) functions primarily as a transition chord. Because of the unpleasant tritone interval, the listener's mind does not want to remain focused on the seventh chord for long. It wants to move on or *resolve* to a more pleasant sound.

Play a D7 chord. Notice the tension. Now play a G major chord. Aah . . . ! In the G chord can be felt a release of the tension created by the D7 chord. This is how seventh chords work to create movement within a chord progression. In a chord change from D major to G major, more excitement can be created if you change the last measure or two of the D major to a D7. Play the following chord progression:

$$D - D - G - G$$

Substitute the second measure of the D chord with a D7, and you will hear the more pronounced sense of movement:

$$D - D7 - G - G$$

The seventh chord not only creates movement, it creates *predictable* movement. Because of the internal dynamics of the chord, the dominant seventh chord leads four positions up the musical alphabet. For example, the D7 chord leads four positions up to a G-rooted chord (D, E, F, G). By "G-rooted" chord we mean any chord that uses a G note as its naming note. It may be a G major, a G minor, a G7, etc. A G7 chord leads four notes up the musical alphabet to a C-rooted chord(G,A,B,C).

This idea is very important when trying to figure out progressions by ear. When your ear tells you that the "mystery chord" is a seventh-type chord, you have a clue as to the probable root name of the next chord! Count four degrees up the musical alphabet to determine the root name of the next chord. To identify the mystery chord's type, listen to the emotional characteristics and degree of consonance or dissonance.

Though diatonically speaking, the seventh chords usually appear as the 2, 3 or 6 chord, *any* chord can be voiced as a seventh when it is used to signal movement up a fourth. For example, though the G chord is commonly played as a major type in the key of G major, it can be voiced as a G7 when it is followed by a C chord. Similarly, the D chord can be voiced as D7 chord when followed by a G chord. A C chord can be voiced as a C7 when it precedes an F.

The chord function probability chart is reprinted below for your convenience. If you are having trouble guessing a particular chord by the probability method alone, you can use its *type* as a clue as to its *function,* revealing its probable *name.*

Just as we can devise a probability chart based on chord function, we can also devise a probability chart based on chord type. We learned that the basic three chords are most commonly voiced as major types. Therefore, in the key of G, if you determine that a chord is of a major type, it is likely a G, D or C chord, in that order of probability.

We also learned that the diatonic supporting chords are often minor or seventh types. This means that if you determine that a certain unknown chord is of the minor type, it is likely an E, A or B chord, in that order of probability.

If the unknown chord is a seventh chord, it can be an A7, E7 or B7 chord, in that order of probability. Remember, a seventh chord can also be a G, C or D chord if it is followed by a chord that is a fourth higher — sometimes it is necessary to go one chord further in the progression to find clues that will help you identify a chord.

Remember, in music forms that feature the five-string banjo, the supporting chords are often played as major types. Therefore, if an unknown chord is determined to be a major type but does not seem to be either a G, C or D chord, guess A, E or B, in that order.

Use the chord type probability chart below to guide your guesses or double-check a progression that you could not figure out entirely using the chord function probability chart.

Chord Function Probability Chart — Key of G Major

G, D, C, A (Am or A7), E (Em or E7), F, B (B7 or Bm), B-flat

Most-used chords   Least-used chords

Chord Type Probability Chart — Key of G Major

If a chord is of the major type, guess the following, in this order of probability:

G D C A E F B B-flat

If a chord is of the minor type, guess the following, in this order of probability:

Em Am Bm Cm Gm Dm

If a chord is of the seventh type, guess the following, in this order of probability:

D7 A7 G7 C7 E7 B7 F7

For an in-depth study of chord theory, purchase *How to Play by Ear* by Jack Hatfield. See ad page in the back of this book.

Chapter 2

FAKING A SOLO

You have probably seen banjoists who are able to play a song that they have never heard before in a jam session. The term sometimes applied to this ability is *faking*. Though the term implies cheating or playing something less than acceptable, it is a valid and useful skill that allows the musician to remain an active part of the group instead of having to sit out on an unfamiliar song. More importantly, the faked solo is a basic foundation upon which a more accurate rendition can be constructed. It can also be used as a viable roll backup to enhance the lead part.

The ability to instantly play a song seems amazing to those of limited experience. How does one play a song he has never performed without referring to a written solo or working out an arrangement beforehand? He bases his playing solely on the chords to the song. It is a simple matter to watch another musician's left hand or have the chords called out. There are literally dozens of songs that have the same or similar progressions. Because of this, and because he knows the probabilities explained in Chapter 1, the experienced musician can frequently guess the upcoming chord in a given situation. If he has heard the song before, he may be able to play all or most of the chords from memory, even though he has never actually worked out an arrangement. Each time he repeats the song, he becomes more familiar with the melody, altering his note choices to render that melody more accurately. Eventually the faked solo becomes an accurate rendition of the melody.

To fake a solo by ear, simply hold the proper chords at the proper time while playing basic right hand patterns. The following version of the forward roll is effective because it allows access to the root note on the first beat of the measure, no matter which chord is being played. Therefore, you can play simple faked solos with only one right hand sequence.

FORWARD ROLL

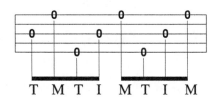

If we combine left hand chord positions with the forward roll, we can construct some generic patterns that can be inserted into any measure of G, C or D (or D7).

ONE-MEASURE G	ONE-MEASURE C	ONE-MEASURE D (or D7)

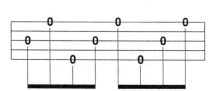 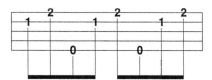 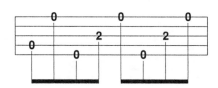

In order to use these patterns to truly play a song by ear, you will have to learn to play them "on the fly". Spend a few minutes memorizing these patterns, then try combining them at random. Try to reach the point that you can combine them in a seamless arrangement, with no hesitation between patterns. To compose a faked solo using these patterns, simply insert the appropriate pattern into the chord progression.

A faked solo for the sample song *Worried Man Blues* appears on the following page to demonstrate the procedure:

Worried Man Blues - Faked Solo

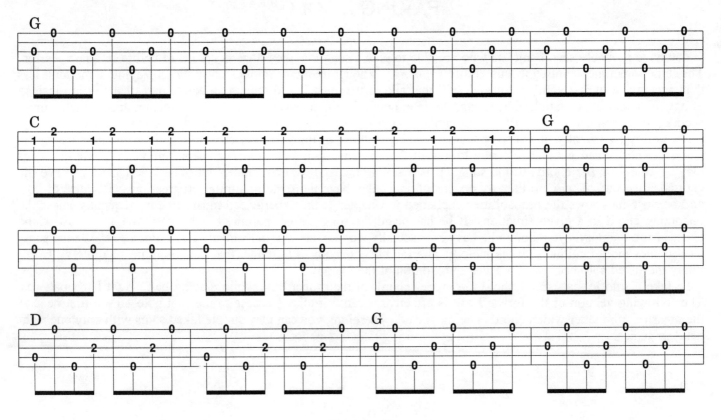

Exercise 8

FAKING SOLOS BASED ON "BASIC THREE" PROGRESSIONS

Using the appropriate patterns, construct a faked solo for the progression of Sample Song #1 which you learned in Chapter 1. Play your faked solo along with the recording to check your work. Use the blank tablature below to record your arrangement if desired. The chords are provided above the tablature. *The answer arrangement appears on page 98.*

Progression #1

G

D

G   C

G   D   G

Using Phrasing Licks

When writing, we use commas to signal a pause at the end of a phrase or to break up a sentence into easy-to-understand segments. We use periods to signal the end of the sentence. Just as we speak and write in phrases, we also play music in phrases. Each song, even if it is an instrumental, has its musical clauses and sentences.

In three-finger banjo, we have specific licks that act as musical commas and periods. Two of the most popular are the *fill roll* and the *pinch*. Though they are interchangeable, the fill roll generally denotes a less pronounced pause, like taking a breath between phrases, and the pinch is more final, like the end of a sentence.

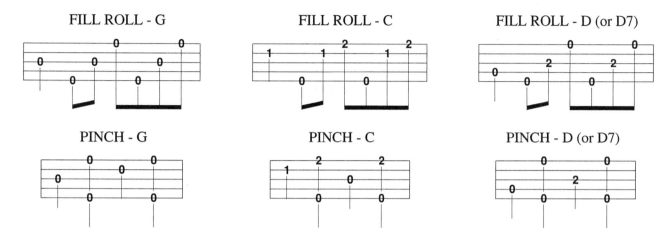

The tag lick is a very definite "period" that appears at the end of banjo "sentences". It is used at the end of complete phrases or where a fill lick of longer than one measure is required. It almost always occurs at the end of a song part. The tag lick occupies five beats. The remaining three beats can be a roll, a pinch, or pickup notes leading to the next melody note.

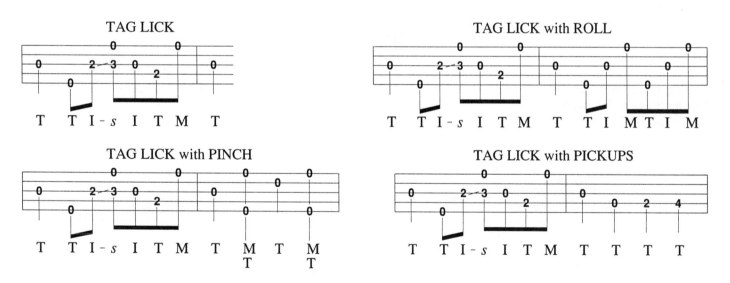

Listening to the Banjo Player

Up to this point we have dealt with learning chord progressions and faking solos by listening primarily to the rhythm instruments. Of course, many of the songs you learn by ear will also include vocal parts which will give you clues. It is fair to assume that most of the recordings you will be learning from will include a banjo part. Though duplicating the banjo player's notes exactly may be too difficult right now, you *can* listen to the banjo player to get a general idea of how to interpret the song. You can especially learn about the phrasing by listening for the pinches, fill rolls and tag licks in the existing banjo part.

Listen again to the sample song *Worried Man Blues* on the recording and try to identify the phrases. On the following page a revised version of the song is shown, with phrasing licks inserted in the appropriate locations.

Worried Man Blues - Phrasing Licks Added

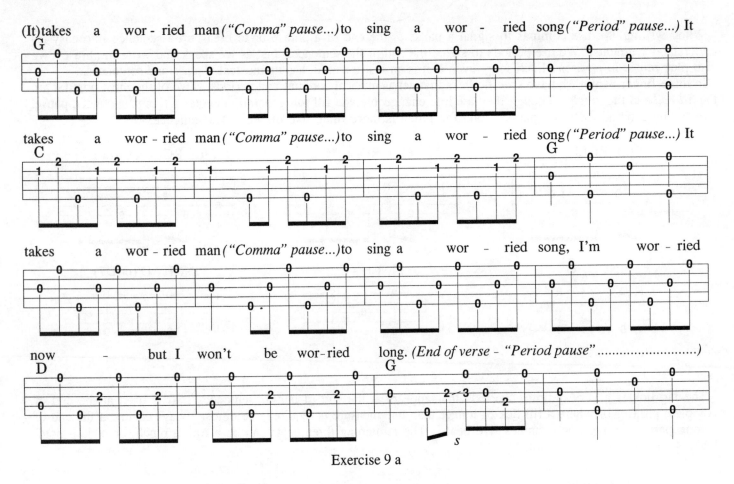

(It)takes a wor - ried man *("Comma" pause...)* to sing a wor - ried song *("Period" pause...)* It

takes a wor - ried man *("Comma" pause...)* to sing a wor - ried song *("Period" pause...)* It

takes a wor - ried man *("Comma" pause...)* to sing a wor - ried song, I'm wor - ried

now - but I won't be wor-ried long. *(End of verse - "Period pause" ....)*

Exercise 9 a

USING PHRASING LICKS

Listen again to Song Example #1 on the recording. Revise the arrangement you created on page 28, inserting the phrasing licks in the proper locations. The blank tablature below can be used to record your arrangement. *A sample answer appears on page 98.*

Progression #1

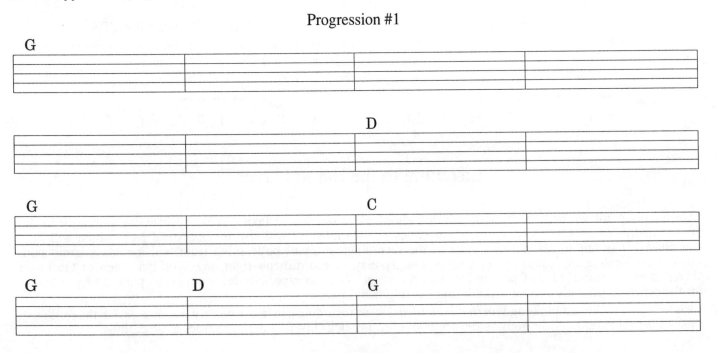

Listen to the progression of Song Example #2 on the recording. Create a faked solo, complete with phrasing licks. Record your arrangement below. *Though there is no one correct answer, a sample answer appears on page 99.*

Progression #2

Verse:

G

D   G

D   G

Chorus:

C   G

C   G   D

G

D   G

Faking Solos Based on Quickly Changing Progressions

At times two chords may appear within one measure. Usually when this occurs, the measure is divided evenly, each chord occupying two beats (in 4/4 time). In order to access the first beat of both chords with the thumb, two-beat rolls such as the alternating thumb roll are useful. Two two-beat rolls with fit into one measure of 4/4 time.

ALTERNATING THUMB ROLLS

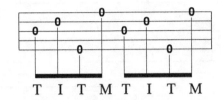

T   I   T   M   T   I   T   M

Sample measures are shown below, using alternating thumb rolls to fill the most commonly occurring two-chord measures.

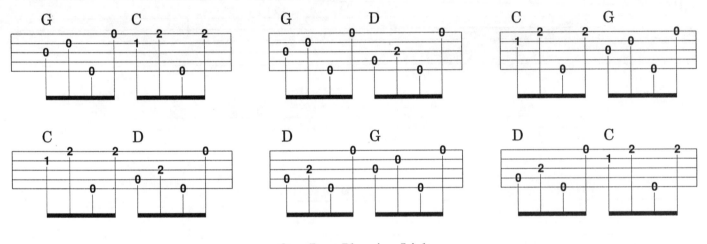

One-Beat Phrasing Licks

Often when the chords change within the measure, a phrase-ending melody note will occur on the third beat of the measure, and a fill will be needed on the fourth beat — a fill that will not be mistaken for the melody note. The following fill licks occupy one beat, but they do not involve the inside strings, where the melody is usually found. The first two can be considered "comma licks" — they signify a pause in the melody, but not necessarily the end of a phrase. The third lick, the pinch, can be considered a "period lick" — it suggests a greater sense of finality (though these licks are often used interchangeably).

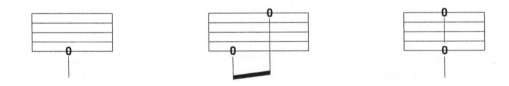

The popular banjo tune *Cripple Creek* is an example of a song with a quickly changing progression. A sample faked solo is shown on the following page, complete with one-beat phrasing licks.

Cripple Creek

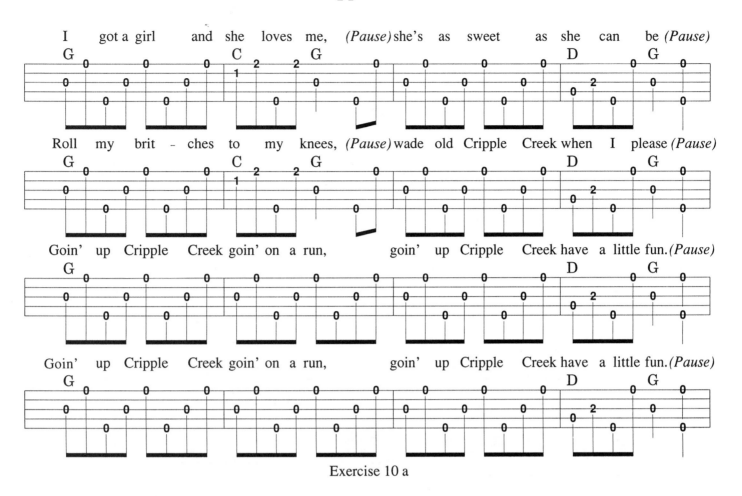

Exercise 10 a

FAKING A SOLO BASED ON A QUICKLY CHANGING PROGRESSION

Construct a faked solo for the quickly changing progression of Song Example #4 on the recording. *Though there is no one correct answer, a sample answer appears on page 100.*

Song Example #4

G
                                       G   D

G
                                         D   G

G
                                         D   G

G
                                         D   G

FAKING A SOLO BASED ON A QUICKLY CHANGING PROGRESSION

Construct a faked solo for the quickly changing progression of Song Example #5 on the recording. *Though there is no one correct answer, a sample answer appears on page 100.*

Song Example #5

Verse:

G   G   C   G   G   D

G   G   C   G   D   G

Chorus:

G   D   G

G   D   G

Use the blank tablature below for notes or as a workspace to construct other solos.

Faking a Solo in 3/4 Time

When faking a solo in 3/4 time, the same principles apply as in 4/4 time. The various roll patterns are simply modified by omitting two notes from the forward rolls or adding two notes to the alternating thumb roll. These modified rolls are shown below.

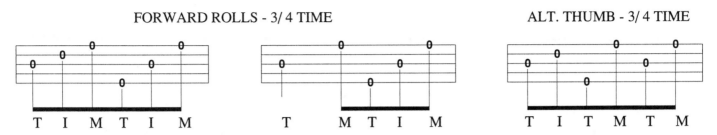

FORWARD ROLLS - 3/4 TIME   ALT. THUMB - 3/4 TIME

T   I   M   T   I   M   T   M   T   I   M   T   I   T   M   T   M

Using these rolls as a basis, we can construct some "generic" patterns that can be plugged into any chord progression that consists of G, C and D (or D7).

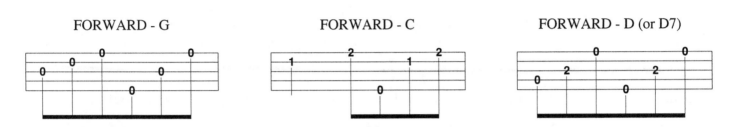

FORWARD - G   FORWARD - C   FORWARD - D (or D7)

For quickly changing chord situations, the four-note alternating thumb roll can be especially useful, as it lets the thumb access any downbeat. This allows for the sounding of the root note on the first beat of the new chord, no matter which beat it occurs on.

Note–In 3/4 time, the second chord in a two-chord measure almost always occurs on the third beat of the measure:

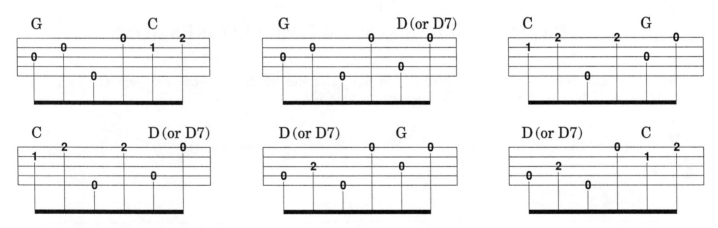

Various phrasing licks, altered for use in 3/4 time, are shown below:

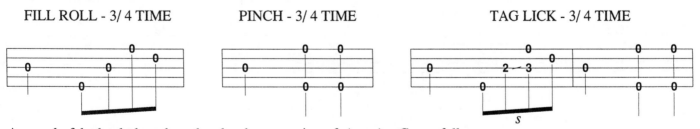

FILL ROLL - 3/4 TIME   PINCH - 3/4 TIME   TAG LICK - 3/4 TIME

A sample faked solo based on the chord progression of *Amazing Grace* follows.

35

Amazing Grace - Faked Solo

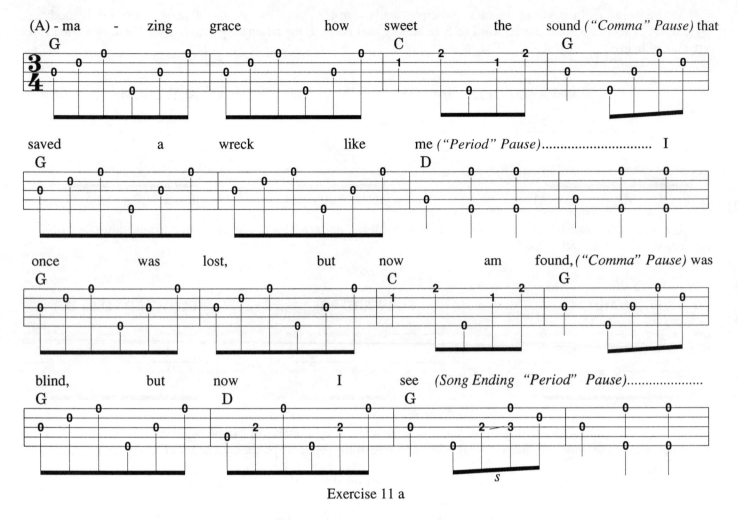

(A) - ma - zing grace how sweet the sound *("Comma" Pause)* that
saved a wreck like me *("Period" Pause)*............................. I
once was lost, but now am found, *("Comma" Pause)* was
blind, but now I see *(Song Ending "Period" Pause)*.....................

Exercise 11 a

FAKING SOLOS BASED ON 3/4 TIME PROGRESSIONS

Construct a faked solo based on the progression of Song Example #3. Record your arrangement on the blank tablature below if desired. *A sample answer appears on page 101.*

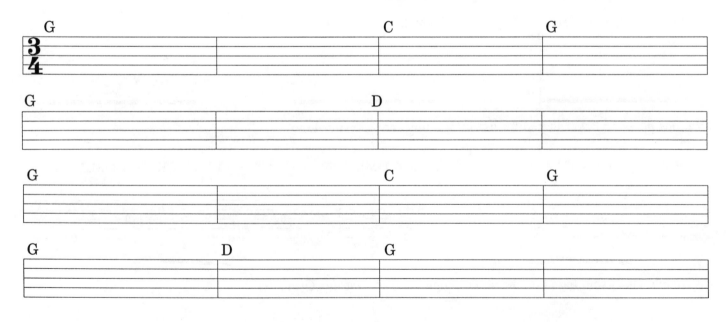

Exercise 11 b

Construct a faked solo for the quickly changing progression of Song Example #6. Record your arrangement on the blank tablature below if desired. The chords are provided. *Though there is no one correct answer, a sample answer appears on page 101.*

Sample Song #6 — Faked Solo

G   C   G   D   G

$\frac{3}{4}$

D   G   D   G

G   C   G   D   G

Use the blank tablature below for notes or as a workspace to construct other solos.

Faking Solos Based on Complex Progressions

Now we will move on to progressions that contain the 2, 3, 6, and flatted 7-rooted chords, the A, B, E, and F-rooted chords in the key of G. We present them in this order, for this is roughly the order of frequency in which they occur.

Note that some of these chords are often played as minor or seventh chords as well as major types. In order to keep the procedure as simple as possible, the patterns below omit the note in the chord that defines it as major, minor, or seventh. Though you are not sounding this "color" note, each pattern will harmonize with any chord type that is based on the root note indicated.

These patterns sound the root note of the chord on the first beat of the measure and as often as possible within the measure. This helps define the chord changes and produces a clean sound that blends unobtrusively with any coinciding lead part.

Though you are only playing certain strings, hold the full chord formation. If you strike strings other than the ones dictated by the patterns shown, the notes sounded will be valid chord tones and will not clash with the other instruments.

Practice the patterns below until you can play any one of them at will and combine them in any order. Then proceed to Exercise 12.

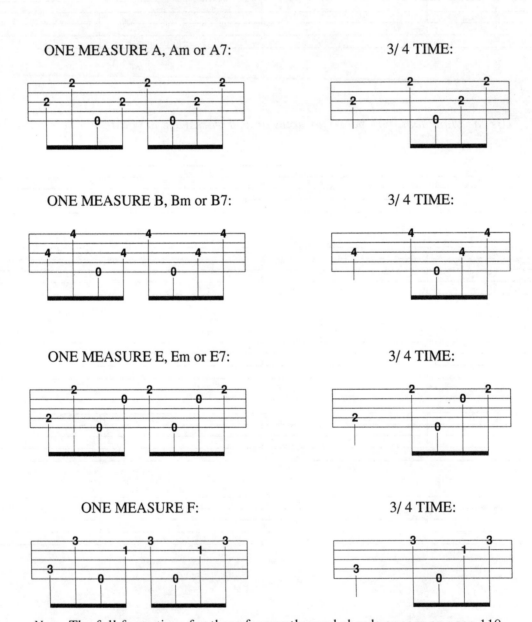

Note—The full formations for these frequently used chords appear on page 119.

FAKING SOLOS BASED ON COMPLEX PROGRESSIONS

Construct a faked solo by ear for each of the progressions below. These are the 4/4 time progressions you learned by ear in Exercise 5 on page 20 and Exercise 6 on page 21. Use the blank tablature that follows to record your arrangement if you desire. *To check your work, play your faked solo along with the recording.*

Exercise 12 a — Progression #7:

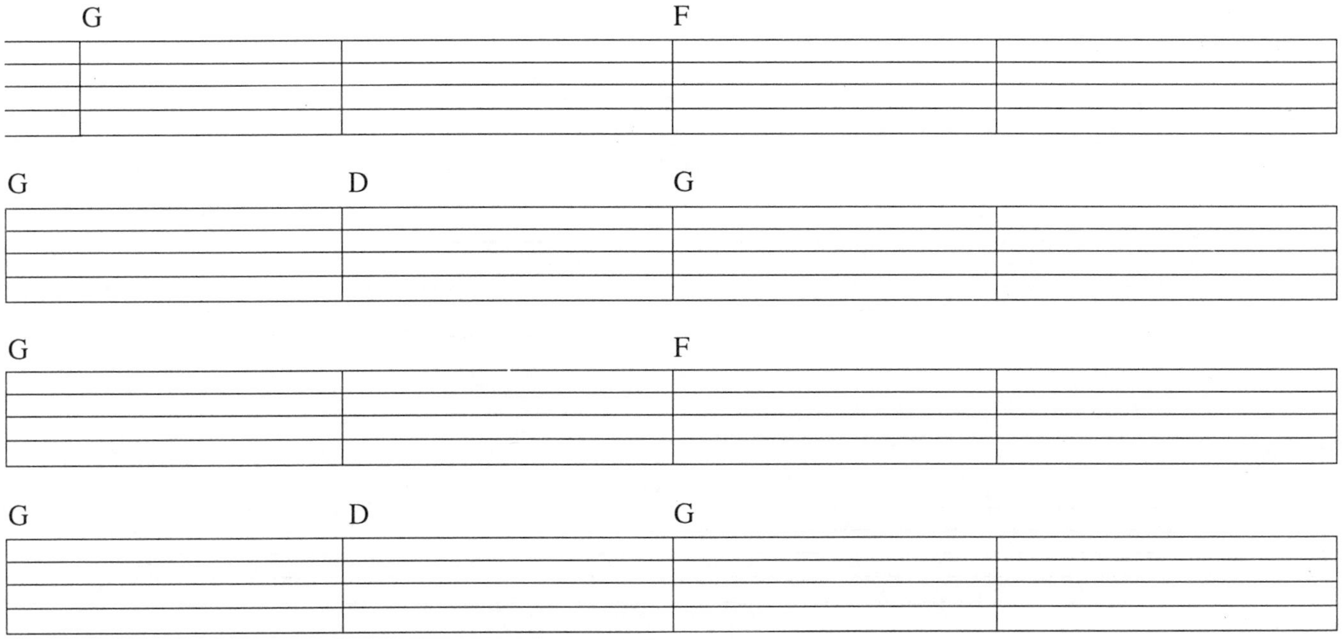

G   F

G   D   G

G   F

G   D   G

Exercise 12 b — Progression #8:

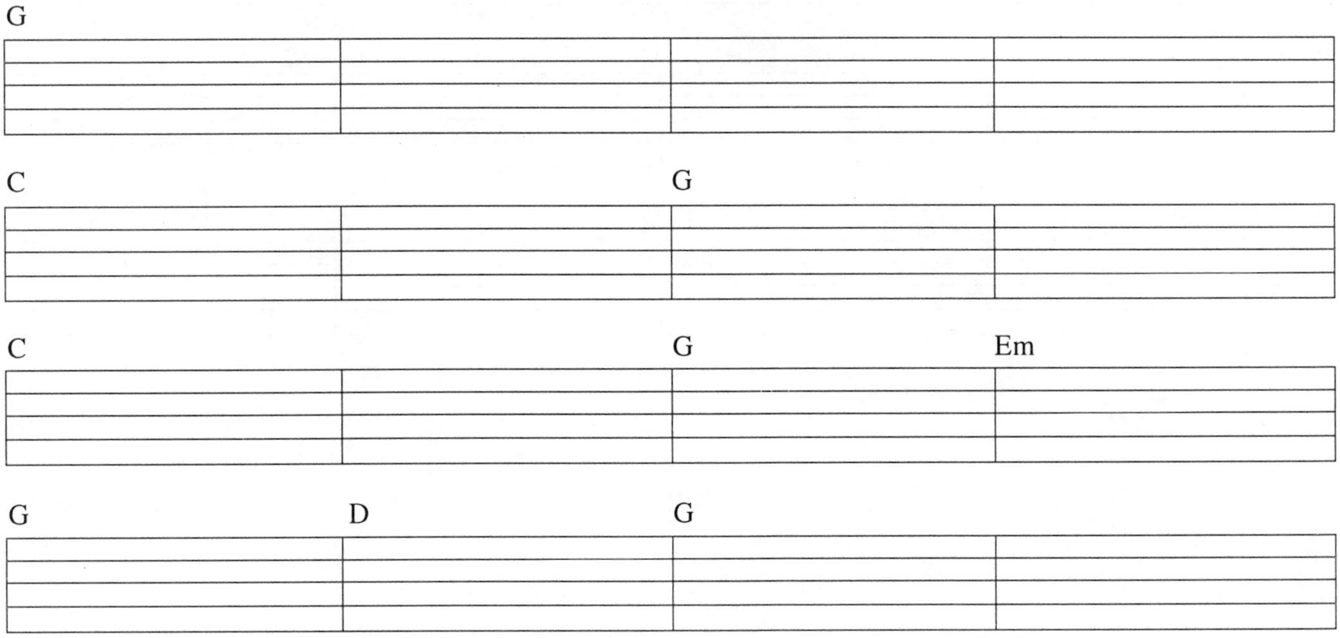

G

C   G

C   G   Em

G   D   G

Verse:

G		C	G

C	G	A	D

G		C	G

C	G	D	G

Chorus:

C		G	

D		G	

C		G	

D		G	

Exercise 12 d — Progression #10:

C   G

C   G

G   B7   C

G   D   G

Exercise 12 e — Progression #11:

G   E   A

D   G

G   E   A

D   G

Exercise 12 f — Progression #12:

G			
		D	
	D7	G	
G			
	G7	C	
C	C♯dim	G	E7
A7	D7	G	

Use the blank tablature that follows for notes or as a workspace to construct other solos.

Chapter 3

PLAYING THE MELODY

In the preceding chapters we laid the groundwork for playing a song by ear. We accomplished this by learning to figure out chord progressions and learning the principle of inserting roll patterns to create a faked solo. We will now learn to create a real melody oriented solo by ear. In order to implement the procedure described in this chapter, however, it will help to have a fundamental understanding of the three-finger style.

The Structure of the Three-Finger Style

Earl Scruggs perfected a style that is not only well suited to the instrument, it is also dynamic and unique. It is a style whose sheer difficulty, especially at the fast tempos of bluegrass music, requires that the number of right-hand patterns be limited. The more right-hand patterns used, the less precise the execution. There must be a balance between using enough right-hand patterns to render any melody accurately, but few enough that they can be played with acceptable speed and accuracy.

The basic concept of three-finger style involves the sounding of *melody notes* by the thumb of the right hand whenever possible. If the thumb is not available because of the finger sequence chosen or because the melody note falls on the first string, the index or middle finger can be used. The spaces between the melody notes are occupied by *fill notes* which maintain the unbroken note flow and provide harmony from the chord tones. The fill notes are secondary in importance to the melody notes, and should be played at a somewhat lesser volume. It is difficult to control the volume of individual notes at the 12 to 15 notes per second sometimes required of the banjoist. The thumb is the strongest digit, and can strike the strings in a downward motion that produces a fuller, louder note. The style dictates that the thumb usually plays on the first downbeat of the measure, and often on the last downbeat. Since these are the locations of the most important melody notes, the emphasis of the melody is somewhat automatic. Because of the tempos involved, the use of the same right-hand finger twice in succession is avoided except after quarter notes and at very slow tempos.

All of these requirements and limitations have led to the evolution of a few specific *rolls* — right-hand finger sequences which can be internalized to the point that they can be played extremely fast. The concept of rolls allows the banjoist to produce several notes with one thought, instead of considering each note separately. This is how the incredible speed mentioned above is attained.

Additional emphasis is placed on important melody notes by the use of *slurs*. Slurs are left-hand techniques such as the *slide, hammer-on* and *pull-off*. Rolls and slurs are combined with certain note choices to produce short recognizable phrases called *licks*. Licks are like interchangeable building blocks that can be combined in various ways to render a melody in three-finger style.

The exercises in Chapter 2 were very important not only in showing you how to fake a solo, but also because they illustrate the concept of using licks as building blocks to construct an arrangement. However, there is one major difference between creating a faked solo and creating an accurate melody oriented solo by ear.

In creating the faked solo, the component licks are chosen based on the chord progression. In creating the melody oriented solo, however, the licks are chosen according to the melody of the song. Do not misunderstand — when playing a melody based solo, awareness of the chord progression is still important. Many of the melody notes are found in the chord. Also, the chord provides fill notes that are harmonious. But in playing a melody oriented solo, the important note choices are dictated by the *melody* as sung or played, not by the chord name. Therefore, you must learn to focus on and be able to duplicate the melody notes before you can truly play a song by ear.

Identifying the Melody

In Chapter 1 you learned to count time and identify the first beat of each measure. The first beat of the measure is important not only because it coincides with most of the chord changes, but also because that is where the most important melody notes occur.

But how do you determine what those melody notes are? In Chapter 2 we formulated a palette of possible chords that may appear. It would help to also have a palette of notes to draw from when guessing the melody. For this, we will look to the *scale* that is the basis of note selection for the melody.

The Scale

The melody notes of a song are almost always derived from the key scale. In the popular key of G major, the key scale is the G major scale. Think of the scale as being a group of "legal" tones that can be used as melody notes. Most melodies draw from no more than one and a half octaves of the scale. This is roughly the range of G scale notes that appear on the first five frets of the banjo. Note that some notes can be found in two locations. This is important, for the right-hand finger sequence may not always allow access to one location, so the other location will be used. Now let us familiarize ourselves with these notes.

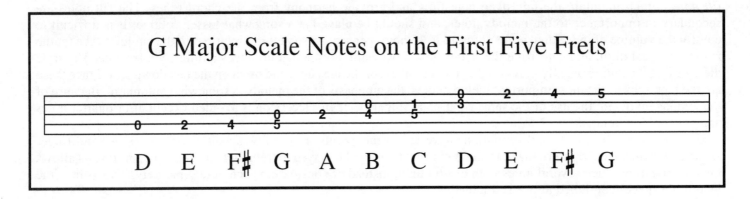

From the open fourth string to the first string at the fifth fret, there are 18 note positions. In selecting the G scale notes as a working palette, we have reduced the number of possible melody notes to only 11. On the next page is a fingerboard diagram that will provide a graphic picture of these notes. Memorize the location of these notes. Except for rare minor or modal phrases and the "grace notes" that accompany slurs, these are the only notes you need to construct most melodies in the key of G major. *Note:* When minor or modal chords are present in the progression, the palette can be expanded to include a few other notes, most notably the F natural and B-flat notes. The F natural note appears on the first and fourth strings at the third fret. The B-flat note appears on the third string at the third fret. If the F chord or the B-flat chord appears in a progression, add these notes to your palette, and expect to hear them in conjunction with these chords.

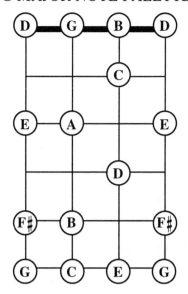

The Trial-and-Error Procedure

The process of learning a melody by ear is one of trial and error. There is no method of learning by ear that will totally replace trial and error. The information and procedures in this book, however, will reduce the guesswork immensely. The keys to playing by ear are to listen very carefully and to gain as much experience as possible. The more you practice listening and guessing melody notes, the more proficient you will become. After much experience, you will be playing by ear almost unconsciously. The hardest part is getting started. Most of the readers of this book already possess the necessary skills, but have simply not sharpened those skills by trying to use them to learn songs by ear. Reading this text will educate you about tendencies of chord progressions. It will inform you of chord and note probabilities. It will teach you a step-by-step procedure and give you many other tips and information. Unfortunately, though, no amount of reading will substitute for actually trying to re-create the music by trial and error. So let's get busy.

Can you sing, hum, or whistle a song? If so, you know it well enough to begin learning it on your banjo by trial and error. Working from memory is easier than working from a recording — it eliminates the tedious task of replaying bits of the recording over and over. It would be best to re-create a few songs from memory first before actually learning one from a recording. To do so, simply choose a melody you can already sing or hum, but one that you do not already play on the banjo. The quality of your singing is not important. If you must sing falsetto or with poor tone to produce the desired note, do not be concerned. If you wish, you can use a capo to attain a key that is comfortable for you to sing the song in, while still thinking of the chords in the key of G. If you are absolutely tone deaf, you can whistle the song. In fact you can merely *think* of the melody, but you will probably have better luck if you produce the sounds aloud.

First learn the chords to the song. You can do this either by utilizing the information in Chapter 1 to figure them out on your own, referring to a songbook, or asking somebody to teach you. Work only in the key of G for now. Not only will it be easier to relate the chosen song to the information in this book, but it will also give you valuable practice in the most preferred key for three-finger style banjo players.

Strum the key chord (G) to give yourself a reference tone. Then strum the first chord of the song if it is a chord other than G. Sing or hum the first few notes of the melody to get your bearings. Then sing or hum *only* the first note. Refer to the palette of G scale notes. Using pure trial and error, guess the location of the first melody note using your banjo to sound the guessed note. It is very likely that the melody note is one of the chord tones, especially if the "mystery note" occurs on the first beat of a measure. Since there are only three notes in most of the chords you play, this narrows down the choices considerably. Hold the chord and play the chord tones one at a time, comparing them to the note just sung to see if any of them are indeed the "mystery note".

Play the note you believe to be the "mystery note" and ask yourself if it is higher, lower, or the same pitch as the note you sang or hummed. If it is the correct note, pat yourself on the back and proceed to the next note. If it is too high or too low in pitch, ask yourself *how much* too high or low it is, and select a note from the G scale palette that seems to be closer to the correct pitch. After you have identified the second note of the song, go back and play both notes, singing along to check your guesswork.

Proceed until you have re-created an entire phrase. *Hint* — most phrases are either two or four measures in length. At this point, you may wish to write the phrase in tablature so you will not forget it. Then proceed to the next phrase. Be sure to pay attention to the progression, strumming the proper chord as you sing the melody notes. When you come to a chord change, strum the new chord first, then hum the "mystery note". Hearing the chord will help direct your voice to the proper pitch and give you a better overall impression of the phrase you are working on.

Be sure to listen for repetition. Listen not only to the individual notes but also to the larger song segments. Most songs have at least one melody phrase that occurs twice or even three times, repeating exactly or very closely. In an 8-measure song part, there are usually four 2-measure phrases. In a 16-measure song part, look for four 4-measure phrases. Sometimes as many as three of these four phrases may have the same or a similar melody line. In many songs, the melody line of the entire chorus is exactly like that of the verse — only the lyrics and the vocal harmony are different. Often the first part of the verse and chorus are identical, but they end differently. If you can learn to recognize repetition, you can cut down your learning time by more than half in most songs.

After you have finished, play the song from start to finish, singing along to check your guesswork. If you find errors, rework the problem spots, always listening for repetition.

This is the essence of playing by ear. Though it may seem difficult at first, the trial-and-error procedure is absolutely necessary if you are going to truly learn by ear. The exercise that follows will give you some valuable practice in learning songs by ear from memory. Children's songs are chosen because they are known by all and because they tend to have simple, short melodies and frequent repetition of phrases.

IDENTIFYING SIMPLE MELODY LINES

Use the trial-and-error procedure to learn the melodies of the following songs by ear. Chords are provided. Write the melody on the blank tab, using an erasable pencil. It is not absolutely necessary to include timing stems, though your melody notes should appear in the proper segments of the proper measures. *Answers can be found on page 106.*

Mary Had a Little Lamb

G	G	D	G

G	G	D	G

This Old Man (Knick-Knack, Paddy Whack)

G	G	G	D

G	G	G	D G

Skip to My Lou

G	G	D	D

G	G	D	G

Learning Songs by Ear from Recordings

Now we will begin to learn songs by ear, using a recording as a source. Once you are comfortable with learning a memorized melody using the trial-and-error procedure, learning a melody from a recording is only slightly more difficult. Again, we will use the trial-and-error procedure and the G scale note palette. But this time, we are going to work the procedure in a way that will allow us to later create an arrangement in three-finger style.

Instrumental Introductions, Turnarounds and Solos

Usually a vocal song will start with an instrumental introduction consisting of a full or partial solo or a short phrase known as a *turnaround*. A turnaround usually consists of a G - D - G - G progression or a D - D - G - G progression. Disregard instrumental intros, turnarounds and solos for now. Concentrate on learning the melody strictly from the vocal part. Learning instrumental parts accurately by ear is something that will come much easier after first dealing with the techniques and information described later in this book.

Pickup Notes

Most songs do not start neatly on the first beat of the measure, as do the children's songs on the previous page. In order to identify the first beat of the first full measure so we will have a viable starting point, we must learn to identify and count *pickup notes.*

Pickup notes occur at the very beginning of the song, before the chord progression starts. They will almost always occupy less than a full measure. The pickup notes are often actual melody notes that are sung by the vocalist. In the song *Will the Circle Be Unbroken,* the notes that occur on the first two words are pickup notes. Listening to a band performing this song, you will notice that the music has a noticeable pulse on the first syllable of the word "circle", and every four beats after that. This pulse marks the first beat of each measure. All the chord changes in this song occur on the first beat of a measure. Count along ("**One**, two, three, four... **One**, two, three, four... etc...) to get the feel of where the first beat of each measure is. When the song repeats, notice on what count the pickup notes occur. In the following example, they occur on the beats of three and four:

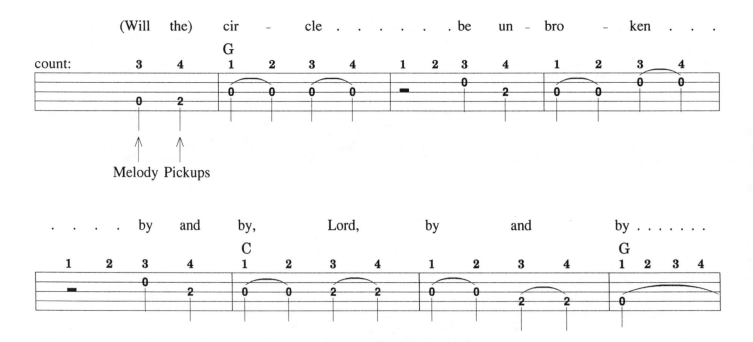

Often the first melody note does occur on the first beat of the measure, but instrumental pickup notes are also used prior to this. This is to signal the rhythm instruments when to begin and to fill up the space between song parts. Non-melody pickup notes are fairly easy to discern in a vocal song. Though there will be introductory notes played by an instrumentalist, no words will be sung on the non-melody pickup note(s). The song *Two Dollar Bill* is a good example. Note that in this arrangement there are three pickup notes that "lead" to the first actual melody note.

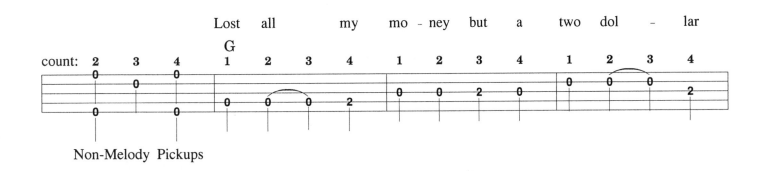

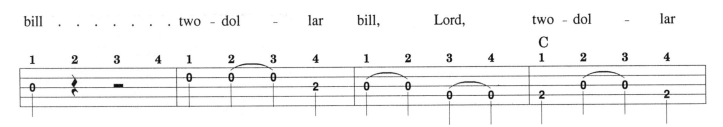

Sometimes the first word or two of the lyrics are indeed pickup notes, but there is also a pickup note or notes played by the instrumentalist prior to these lyrical pickup notes. The song *Mountain Dew* as arranged below is an example.

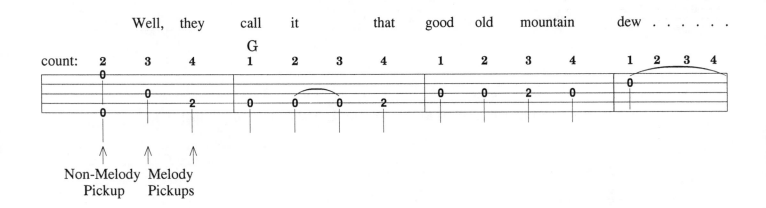

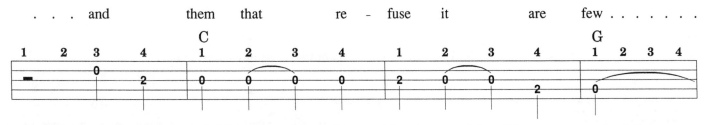

There is no standard number of pickup notes, but the last partial measure and the pickups must equal a full measure. All beats must be accounted for, whether by actual notes or rests. Remember, the starting point of the rhythm instruments marks the first beat of the first full measure. Any notes played and/or sung prior to this are pickup notes.

Listed below are some common pickup note sequences, followed by the melody note that they commonly lead to. Play each sequence a few times and learn to recognize the sound of it. In recognizing one of these sequences in a song you are learning by ear, you will automatically know the first melody note of the first full measure. You will then have a reference point from which to begin the trial-and-error procedure.

PICKUPS LEADING TO G MELODY NOTE (The first chord is usually G)

PICKUPS LEADING TO HIGH D MELODY NOTE (The first chord is usually G or D)

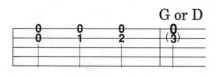 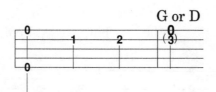 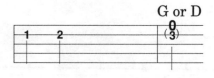

PICKUPS LEADING TO LOW D MELODY NOTE (The first chord is usually G or D)

 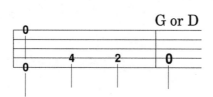 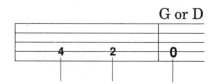

PICKUPS LEADING TO C MELODY NOTE (The first chord is usually C)

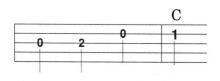 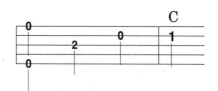 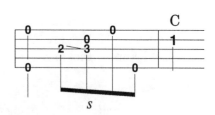

NON-LEADING PICKUPS (The first chord can be any chord in the key)

 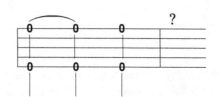 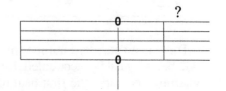

52

Endings

When the song has been completed, there will almost always be a short instrumental phrase known as an *ending* or *tag*. This lick is different from the tag lick, which signifies the end of a phrase or song part within the song proper. Endings are, of necessity, usually one of a few easily recognizable generic phrases. The easiest way to identify an ending is to simply study the examples that follow, playing them on your banjo a few times to become familiar with them. You will then recognize them when you hear them in a song.

ENDING #1

This ending consists of merely brushing the strings to produce a strum. It can follow the last melody note sung or it can follow a tag lick which begins on the last melody note sung. It can be used to end a vocal or instrumental tune.

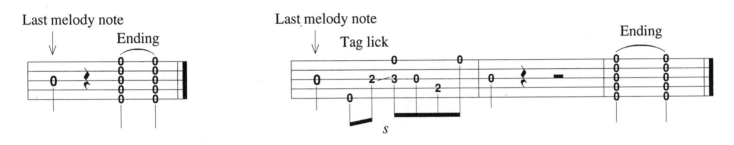

ENDING #2

This ending starts on the last melody note sung. It is virtually always used as an ending in a vocal song.

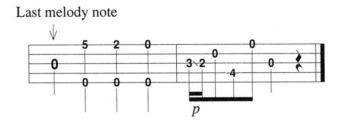

ENDING #3

This ending can occur in a vocal or instrumental tune, though it is most often used on up-tempo instrumentals.

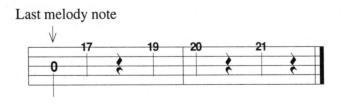

ENDING #4

Last melody note

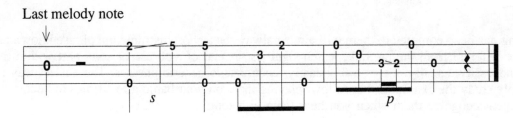

The following ending is of the "shave and a haircut" form. There are several variations of this ending, but they all have the same rhythm as the spoken phrase "Shave and a haircut (pause) — six bits". These endings can be found in vocal or instrumental numbers, but are used more often on instrumentals. They can start on the same beat as the last melody note or they can follow a tag lick that starts on the last melody note. Any variation of Ending #4 can be followed by any variation of Ending #5 to form a two-part ending.

ENDING #5

Last melody note

Intro Endings, Turnaround Endings and Tag Line Endings

When a short instrumental intro or a turnaround begins the song, the same phrase is often used as an ending. Another variation is the *tag line* ending, in which the last line of the song is repeated, either vocally or instrumentally (or both). The songwriter may also devise an original ending, which you would learn by ear as you did any other segment of the song, applying the principles taught in this book. Since these are all based on the melody of the song in question, there are not any generic examples to show.

Locating First-beat Melody Notes

Because of the limitations of three-finger style, it is very difficult to sound every melody note. If you play the melody notes that occur on the first beat of each measure, however, you will have an acceptable arrangement. You used the trial-and-error procedure to learn the children's songs on page 49. Simply apply the same procedure to learning the melody notes that appear on the first beat of each measure in the song to be learned.

Start the recording, stopping it immediately after the melody note that falls on the first beat of the first full measure. Using the trial-and-error procedure, identify that melody note and write it down on blank tablature paper, being sure to place it at the beginning of the measure, just after the measure line. Continue until you have identified all first-beat melody notes. This will produce a basic outline of the melody that you can incorporate into the faked solo you learned earlier. The combination of the two arrangements will result in a melody oriented solo.

The trial-and-error procedure is demonstrated on the recording using the sample song *Worried Man Blues*. The resulting tablature arrangement appears on the following page.

Worried Man Blues — First-beat Melody Notes

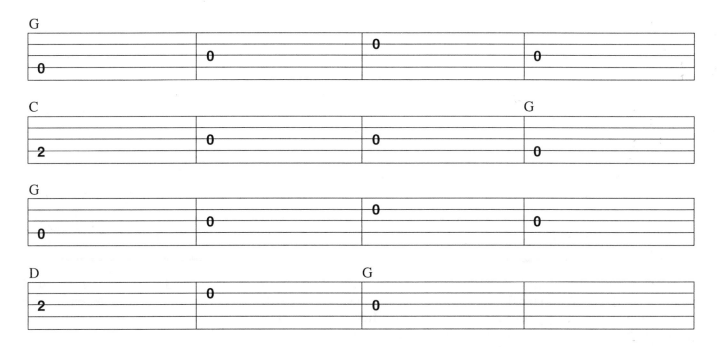

Exercise 14

LOCATING FIRST-BEAT MELODY NOTES

Listen again to Song Example #1. Using the trial-and-error procedure, identify all first-beat melody notes. Record them on the blank tablature below. *The answer arrangement appears on page 107.*

Song Example #1 — First-beat Melody Notes

G

D

G   C

G   D   G

Altering the Faked Solo to Create a Melody Oriented Solo

The faked solos you created in Chapter 2 are already viable arrangements. They contain phrasing licks and fill notes produced from the chord tones. The only thing needed to transform them into melody oriented solos is the melody. This is easily supplied. In the faked solo, replace the existing first-beat notes with the correct first-beat melody note.

Since most melody notes last more than one beat, we also change all other notes that occur on the inside strings to match the first-beat melody note. For example, the first-beat melody note of measure three in *Worried Man Blues* is a B note. We will change all the inside notes from G notes to B notes. The notes on the first and fifth string remain unchanged. These are typically fill notes.

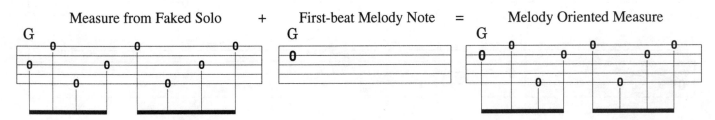

Since you are constructing a melody oriented solo by simply altering the existing faked solo, most of the solo is already learned. The right-hand finger sequences will not change — you will merely play some of the notes on different strings than you originally learned them. The phrasing licks, too, are already memorized. Since they serve the same function in the melody solo as they did in the faked solo, there is no need to alter them except when the first note is changed to render a particular melody note.

The sample song is done for you. The faked solo is presented, then the first-beat melody arrangement. Next the melody oriented solo is created by replacing the inside notes in the faked solo with the same note as the first-beat melody note. Pickups are added to the final arrangement, and final fill notes omitted to make room for the pickups when repeating.

Worried Man Blues - Faked Solo

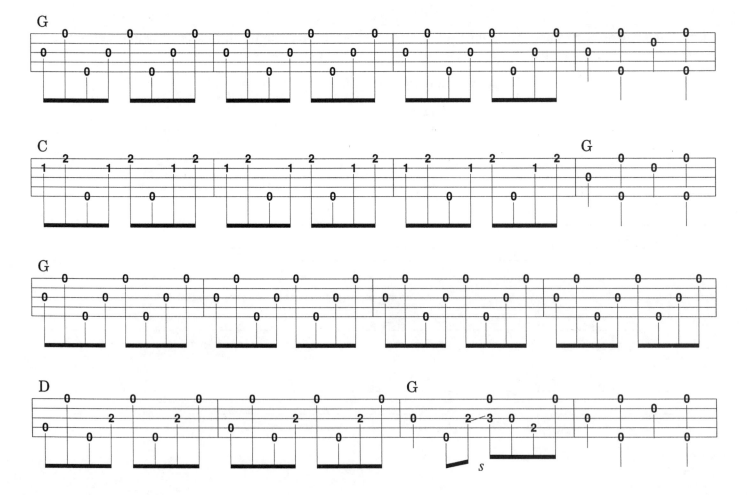

Worried Man Blues - First-Beat Melody Notes

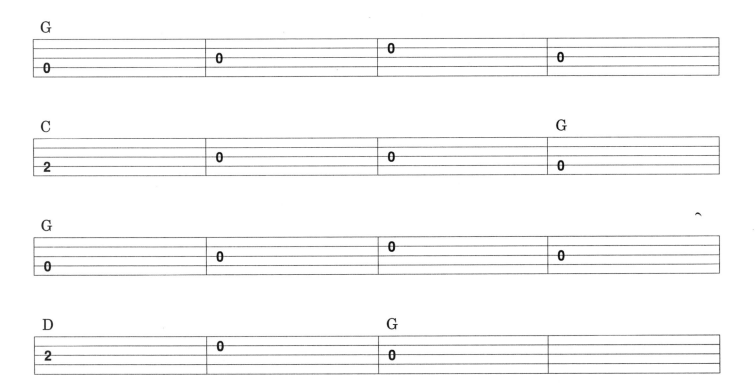

Worried Man Blues-Melody Oriented Solo

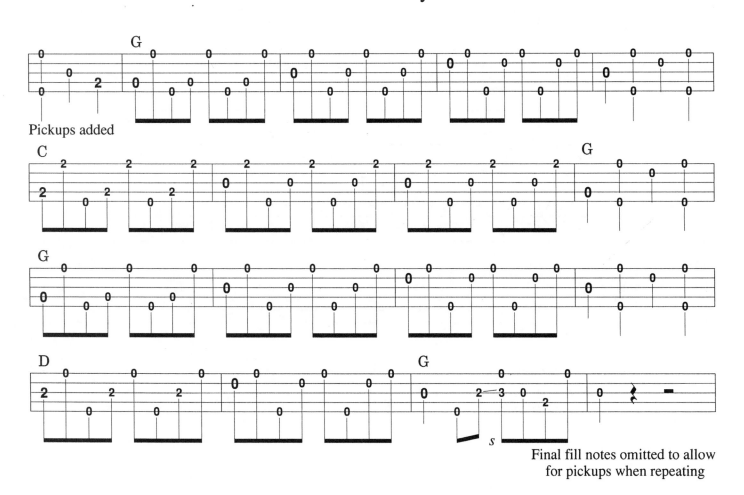

Pickups added

Final fill notes omitted to allow
for pickups when repeating

ALTERING A FAKED SOLO TO CREATE A MELODY ORIENTED SOLO

Alter the faked solo you created for Song Example #1 on page 30 to produce a melody oriented solo. *Though there is no one correct answer, you may compare your arrangement with the sample answer on page 107.*

Song Example #1 — First-beat Melody Notes

G

G   D

G   C

G   D   G

Song Example #1 — Melody Oriented Solo

G

G   D

G   C

G   D   G

Identifying Last-beat Melody Notes

The last downbeat of the measure is also an important location for melody notes. If you can play most of the melody notes that occur on the first *and* last downbeats of each measure, the resulting solo will be very true to the melody. The last-beat melody notes can be identified by the same procedure used to identify first-beat melody notes. After doing so, you will alter the note that falls on the last downbeat of the faked solo accordingly. The third measure of *Worried Man Blues* is used again as an example:

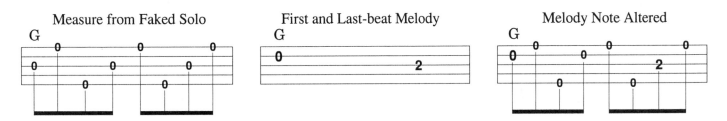

At times the melody note that occurs on the first beat is held throughout the measure. In this situation you merely sound the first-beat melody note throughout the measure:

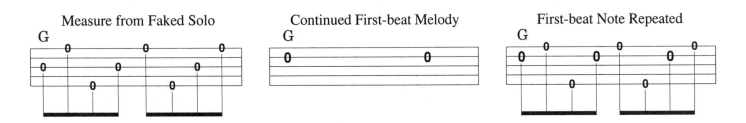

At other times no melody occurs on the last beat. There are two ways to avoid the last-beat note from being incorrectly interpreted as a melody note. One way is to sound a fill note on the last beat. This maintains the note flow without falsely sounding like a melody note. The fill note would typically be a fifth-string note or a pinch. If the finger sequence does not allow the use of the thumb to access the fifth string, another roll can be used that does:

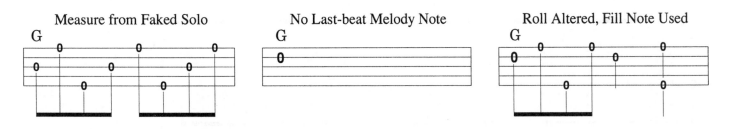

The other way to avoid a mon-melody last-beat note from being incorrectly interpreted as a melody note is to repeat the previous melody note, without emphasizing it. It should be played at the same volume as other fill notes so it is not mistaken for a melody note:

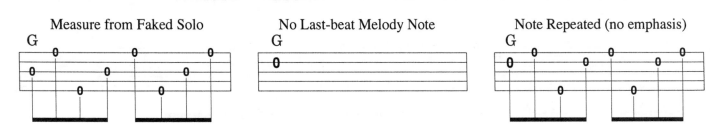

The sample song *Worried Man Blues* is presented below as a first-beat and last-beat melody arrangement, and the first-beat melody oriented solo is shown, altered to include last-beat melody notes.

Worried Man Blues - First-beat and Last-beat Melody Noes

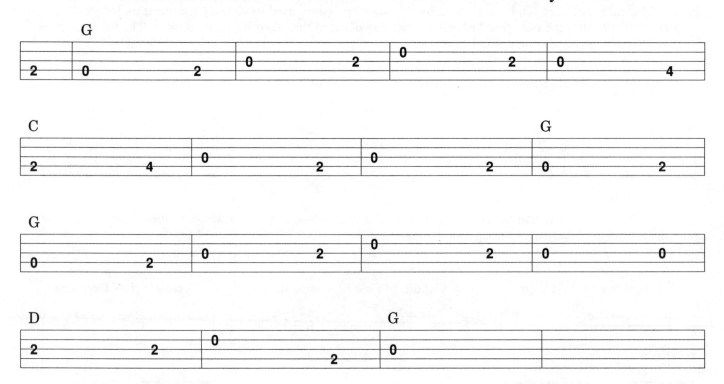

Worried Man Blues - First-beat and Last-beat Melody Oriented Solo

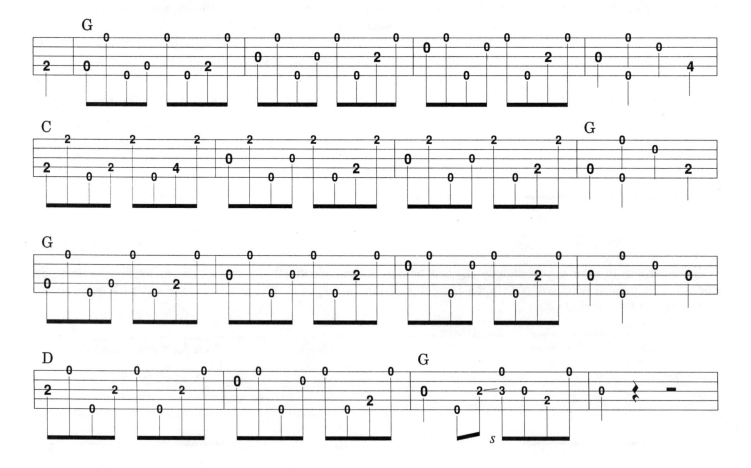

CREATING A FIRST-BEAT AND LAST-BEAT MELODY ARRANGEMENT

Listen again to Song Example #1 on the recording. Identify the melody note that occurs on the last beat of each measure. Modify the melody arrangement you created on page 59 to include last-beat melody notes. Record the altered arrangement on the blank tablature below. *An answer arrangement appears on page 108.* On the following tablature, create a first-beat and last-beat melody oriented solo. *A sample answer appears on page 108.*

Song Example #1 — First-beat and Last-beat Melody

G

G   D

G   C

G   D   G

Song Example #1 — First-beat and Last-beat Melody Oriented Solo

G

D

G   C

G   D   G

Listen again to Song Example #2 on the recording. Identify the melody note that occurs on the first and last beats of each measure. Write the melody notes on the tablature below. *An answer arrangement appears on page 109.* On the following tablature, create a first-beat and last-beat melody oriented solo. *A sample answer appears on page 110.*

Song Example #2 — First-beat and Last-beat Melody

Verse:

G

D   G

G

D   G

Chorus:

C   G

C   G   D

G

D   G

Using the melody arrangement that you created on the previous page, create a first-beat and last-beat melody oriented solo. *A sample answer appears on page 110.*

Song Example #2 — First-beat and Last-beat Melody Oriented Solo

Verse:

G

D   G

G

D   G

Chorus:
C   G

C   G   D

G

D   G

Locating Internal Melody Notes

Though the sounding of the correct melody notes on the first and last beats of the measure will produce a solo that is very accurate by banjo standards, you may wish to continue the process until all accessible melody notes are included in your arrangement. If you used the suggested forward roll pattern, there is a note on one of the inside strings that falls on the second half of the "two" beat. Though the internal melody note will likely occur on the first half of the third beat, it is acceptable in three-finger banjo style to move a melody note forward or backward by half a beat to accommodate the roll pattern chosen.

If you wish to include internal melody notes in your arrangement, simply use the trial-and-error procedure to identify any melody note occurring on or around the third beat, and sound it as the fourth note of the pattern.

Below is a melody arrangement of *Worried Man Blues* with all melody notes included. On the following page is the melody oriented solo with all accessible melody notes incorporated. Note that some internal melody notes are displaced by half a beat to conform to the roll pattern. Note also that some internal melody notes were omitted because they were not readily accessible with the roll pattern chosen.

Worried Man Blues-All Melody Notes

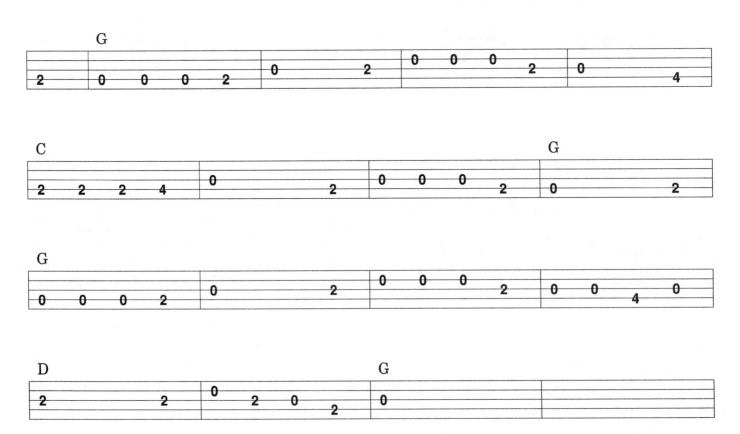

64

Worried Man Blues - Melody Oriented Solo Including All Accessible Melody Notes

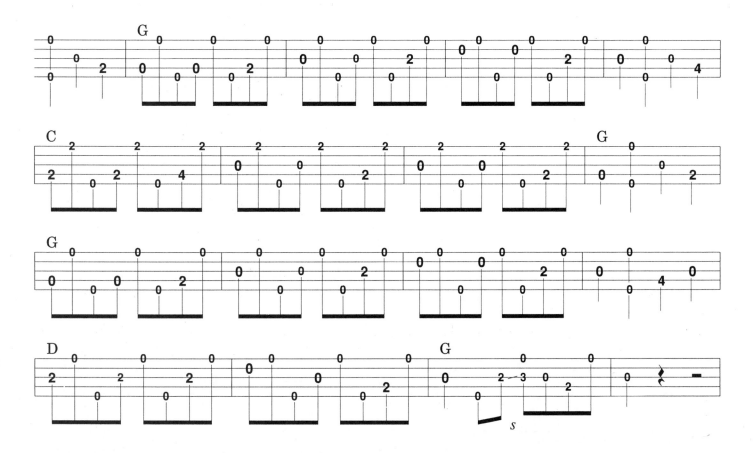

Use the blank tablature that follows for notes or as a workspace to construct other solos.

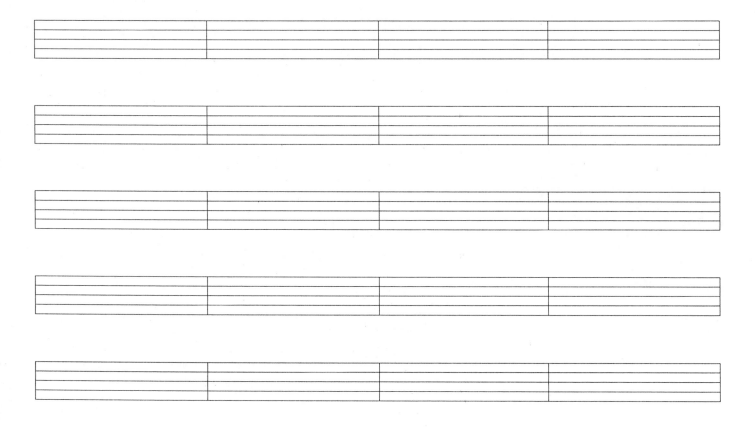

CREATING SOLOS INCLUDING ALL ACCESSIBLE MELODY NOTES

Using the trial-and-error procedure, identify the internal melody notes of Song Example #1. Alter the solo you created on page 61 to include the internal melody notes that can be accessed without altering the rolls. *A sample answer appears on page 111.*

Song Example #1 — All Melody Notes

G

G   D

G   C

G   D   G

Song Example #1 — Melody Oriented Solo with All Accessible Melody Notes

G

G   D

G   C

G   D   G

Identify the internal melody notes of Song Example #2. Alter the solo you created on page 63 to include the internal melody notes that can be accessed without altering the rolls. *A sample answer appears on page 112.*

Song Example #2 — All Melody Notes

Verse:

G

D   G

G

D   G

Chorus:

C   G

C   G   D

G

D   G

Song Example #2 — Melody Oriented Solo with All Accessible Melody Notes

A sample answer appears on page 113.

Verse:

G

D		G	

G

D		G	

Chorus:

C		G	

C		G	D

G

D		G	

Emphasizing the Melody

It has been mentioned that the system of melody notes mixed in among fill notes makes it difficult for some listeners to discern the melody in a three-finger banjo arrangement. There are certain techniques that will help the banjoist to emphasize the melody. One technique, dynamic emphasis, has already been mentioned. The banjoist should always make an effort to play the melody notes with more force than the fill notes. As pointed out earlier, the first-beat melody notes are emphasized somewhat automatically because most rolls start with the more powerful thumb. However, because of the alternation of right-hand fingers required, the index or middle fingers will be required to play some melody notes. Also, the faster the tempo, the more difficult it is to emphasize a melody note with dynamics. Therefore, in order that proper emphasis is placed on all melody notes, other techniques are used by banjoists.

Omitting Fill Notes to Create Quarter Notes

One way to draw attention to a note is to allot it more time. Any eighth note can be transformed into a quarter note simply by omitting the following eighth note. The first note then lasts twice as long, for it occupies the half-beat it originally did, plus the half-beat formerly occupied by the next eighth note.

Since the most important melody notes occupy the *first* half of the first and last beats of the measure, the most commonly omitted fill notes are the ones that occupy the *second* half of the first and last beats of the measure.

An added benefit of omitting the last fill note of a measure is that the banjoist will have an extra half beat to prepare for the note or chord that follows.

ALL EIGHTH NOTES

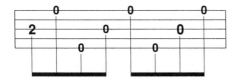

FIRST-BEAT QUARTER NOTE

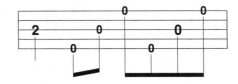

ALL EIGHTH NOTES

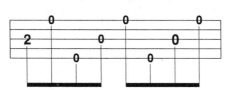

LAST-BEAT QUARTER NOTE

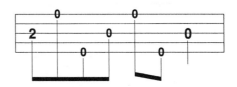

ALL EIGHTH NOTES

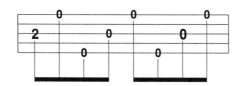

FIRST *AND* LAST-BEAT QUARTER NOTES

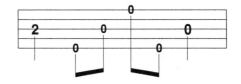

69

The sample song *Worried Man Blues* is shown below with selected first and last upbeats omitted, transforming the previous notes to quarter notes.

Worried Man Blues - Melody Emphasized by Quarter Notes

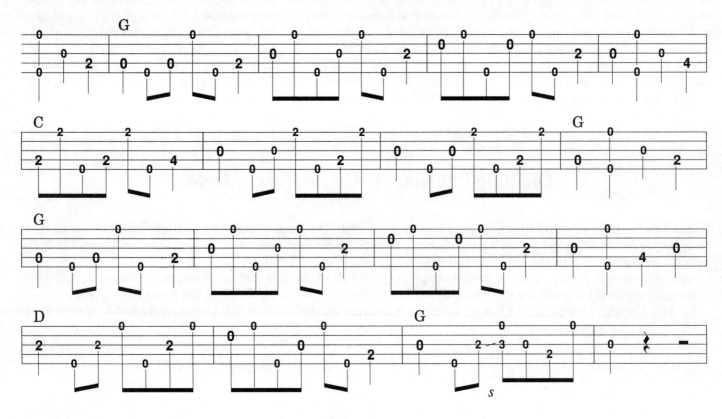

Exercise 18

USING QUARTER NOTES

Alter the melody oriented solo you created for Song Example #1 on page 66, emphasizing the most important melody notes with quarter notes. *Sample answer on page 114.*

Song Example #1 - Quarter Notes Added

G

G   D

G   C

G   D   G

70

Using Slurs

One thing that sets melody oriented solos apart from faked solos and roll backup is the more frequent use of *slurs* — left-hand operations such as hammer-ons, pull-offs, and slides. Slurs usually involve using a left-hand operation to sound two or more notes in the time normally allotted to one eighth note or one quarter note. In addition to emphasizing melody notes, slurs are also used simply to add interest to the music.

If a melody note occurs on an open string, we can locate it instead on the adjacent string as a fretted note. This is necessary in order to perform most slurs.

If a melody note is found on the third string; open (a G note), it can be played instead on the fourth string; fifth fret. If a melody note is found on the second string; open (a B note), it can be played instead on the third string; fourth fret. If a melody note is found on the first string; open (a D note), it can be played instead on the second string; third fret.

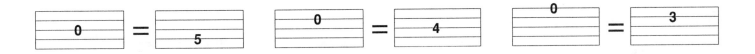

Below are some slurs involving frequently used melody notes. The melody note is usually the *last* note of the slur. You hammer-on, pull-off, or slide *to* the melody note.

HAMMER-ONS to FREQUENTLY USED MELODY NOTES

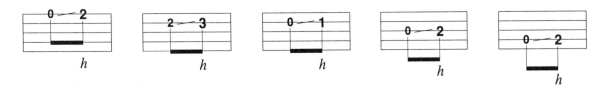

PULL-OFFS to FREQUENTLY USED MELODY NOTES

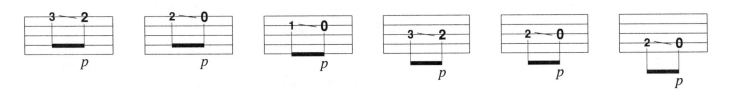

SLIDES to FREQUENTLY USED MELODY NOTES

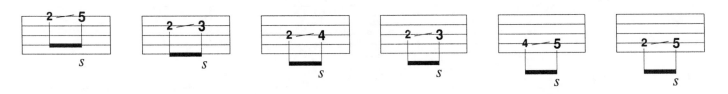

To incorporate slurs into your existing arrangements, simply replace the existing melody note with the two-note slur. *Note* — Use slurs to accent only the most important melody notes, or in places where interest is needed. Use quarter notes also where needed, not only to accent the melody, but also to add rhythmic variation to a long sequence of unbroken eighth notes. Remember also that you can use quarter notes in problem spots, allowing time to "catch up" or to prepare for an upcoming difficult maneuver.

Worried Man Blues - Slurs Added

Exercise 19
ADDING SLURS

Alter the solo you created for Song Example #1 on page 70, emphasizing the melody with slurs. Use no more than two slurs per measure. For a melody note that lasts more than one beat, use the slur only on the initial beat. *Sample answer on page 114.*

Song Example #1 - Slurs Added

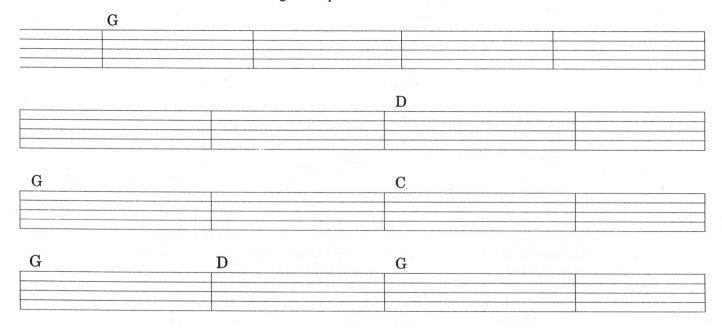

Creating Solos for Quickly Changing Melodies

There are songs whose melody line changes so often that it is necessary to sound many internal melody notes in order to create an acceptable arrangement. These songs may contain passages in which the melody notes occur as often as three or four times per measure. For songs like this, you may have to break the roll at times, sounding two or more consecutive quarter notes, as shown below.

QUICKLY CHANGING MELODY

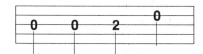

SOLUTION: CONSECUTIVE QUARTER NOTES

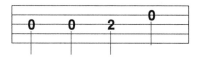

Another way to deal with quickly changing melodies is to use the alternating thumb roll. This roll allows the thumb access to all downbeats.

QUICKLY CHANGING MELODY

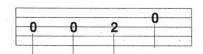

SOLUTION: ALT. THUMB ROLL

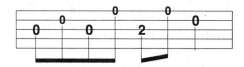

You may use only the first or second half of a standard four-beat roll to access one or two melody notes. Here is an example of how the reverse roll can be divided to form a two-beat roll:

REVERSE ROLL

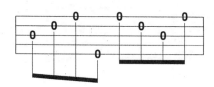

FIRST HALF   SECOND HALF

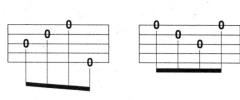

The popular banjo song *Cripple Creek* is a wonderful example of all the techniques discussed above. The melody line appears on the following page, followed by the standard banjo arrangement with techniques labeled.

Cripple Creek - Melody

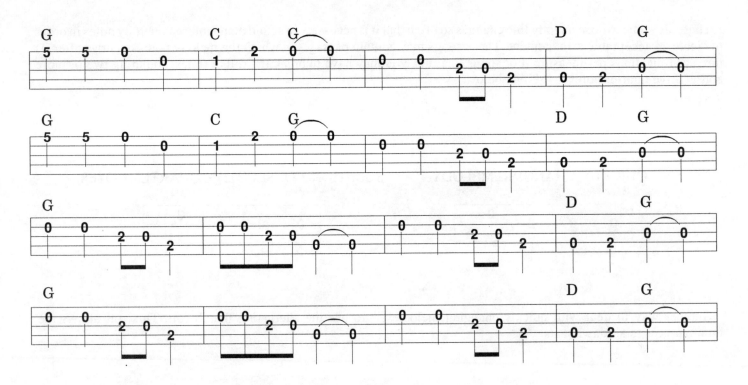

Cripple Creek - Banjo Arrangement

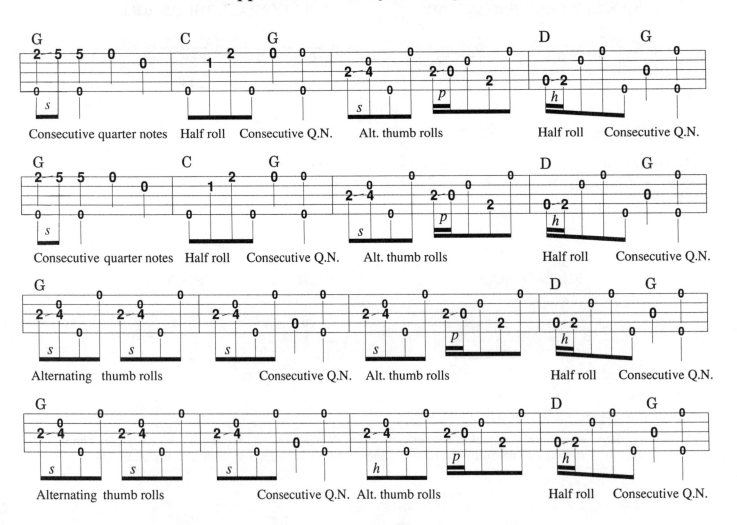

CREATING A QUICKLY CHANGING MELODY SOLO BY EAR

Listen to Song Example #4, which has a quickly changing melody. Learn the melody and record it on the first tablature below. Create a melody oriented solo and record it on the second blank tablature. *Sample answer on page 115.*

Song Example #4 — Melody

G			G	D

G			D	G

G			D	G

G			D	G

Song Example #4 — Melody Oriented Solo

	G			G	D

G			D	G

G			D	G

G			D	G

Listen to Song Example #5, which has a quickly changing melody. Learn the melody and record it on the first tablature below. Create a melody oriented solo and record it on the second blank tablature. *Sample answer on page 116.*

Song Example #5 — Melody

G		G	C	G		G	D

G		G	C	G		D	G

G						D	G

G						D	G

Song Example #5 — Melody Oriented Solo

G		G	C	G		G	D

G		G	C	G		D	G

G						D	G

G						D	G

Creating Melody Oriented Solos in 3/4 Time

To create melody oriented solos in 3/4 time, the principles are the same as described in the preceding pages, except that three-beat rolls will replace four-beat rolls. Below is the melody of *Amazing Grace* followed by a sample melody oriented arrangement to demonstrate the principles involved.

Amazing Grace - 3/ 4 Time Melody

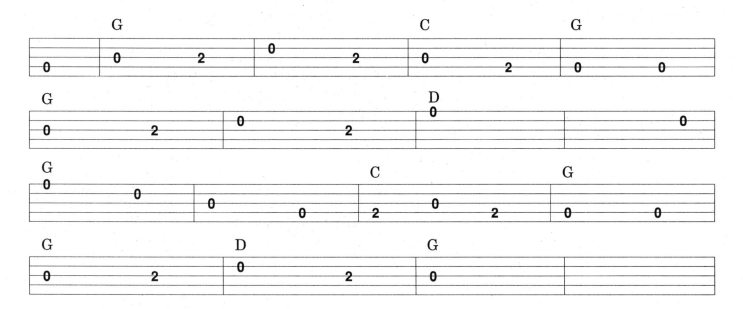

Amazing Grace - Melody Oriented Solo in 3/ 4 Time

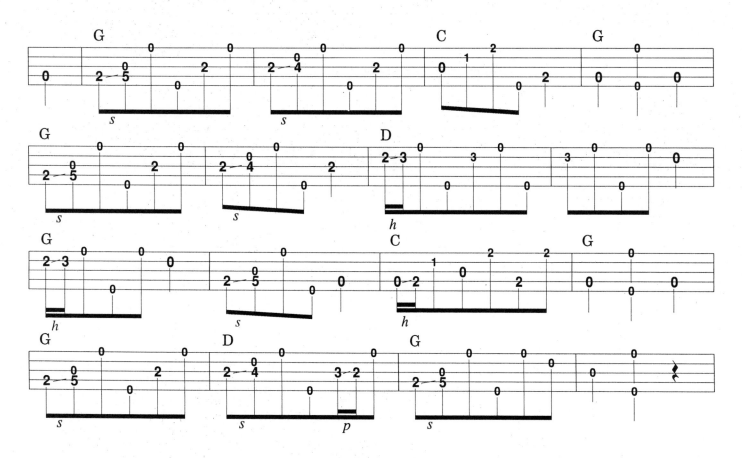

CREATING A MELODY ORIENTED SOLO IN 3/4 TIME

Listen to Song Example #3, which is a 3/4 time melody. Learn the melody and record it on the first tablature below. On the second tablature, combine the melody with the faked solo you created on page 37 to produce a melody oriented solo, complete with quarter notes and slurs. *Though there is no one correct answer, a sample answer appears on page 117.*

Song Example #3 — Melody

G		C	G

G		D	

G		C	G

G	D	G	

Song Example #3 — Melody Oriented Solo

G		C	G

G		D	

G		C	G

G	D	G	

Chapter 4

USING LICKS

If you have worked through the step-by-step procedure presented in this book and applied the principles to new songs, you should now have a pretty good foundation in learning songs on the banjo by ear. Be proud of yourself — being able to reproduce an accurate melody on the five-string banjo is no small accomplishment.

But what about hot licks? You have no doubt heard accomplished banjoists play passages which sound really flashy and show technical skill, but may not bear any resemblance to the melody. You probably already play many of these licks yourself as part of memorized solos, but you may not know how to use them at will.

In a vocal song, the singer sings the melody. The tasteful instrumental soloist will play an initial solo that is very close to the melody line, especially if that solo is an introductory solo. Most songs include at least three verses and choruses and at least two instrumental solos. Even with beautiful singing and perfect instrumental execution, the same melody line repeated ten times in succession may become monotonous. For this reason, the instrumentalist often inserts interesting phrases that bear little or no resemblance to the melody. Later in the song, after the melody has been well established, he may play an entire solo that is not melody oriented, but simply sounds good — one that shows off his skill and the uniqueness of his instrument. The content of this solo will be limited only by the meter and chord progression. The term for this is *improvising.*

You may ask, "What is the difference between improvising and faking?" A faked solo really is improvising, but it occurs because the player is not yet able to play the melody. We will define an improvised solo as one in which the soloist intentionally departs from the melody to make the song more interesting. How would a listener know whether you are improvising or faking? He probably would not be able to tell the difference — but *you* would, and if you want to add some excitement to your playing, you should spend some time learning to improvise.

The building block of the improvised solo is the *lick.* We have defined a lick as a phrase that stands on its own as a musical idea. Licks can be interchanged and combined according to the tastes and ability of the individual player. Every accomplished banjoist has his favorite "signature licks" that he has created himself or adapted from the playing of others. Some original licks are meticulously worked out to fit a certain chord or melody situation. Sometimes licks originate as "happy mistakes" — phrases that were not planned, but sounded good enough for the player to add to his lickabulary. Most licks are learned from recordings, tablature, a teacher, or from other players.

The only way many players can create a solo is to extract licks from their lickabulary and combine them to fit the chord changes. In other words, by faking. Remember, faking is what you do when you do not yet know the melody. Unfortunately, some never progress beyond this stage. It is important to be able to re-create *any* melody at will. Playing strictly from licks, though a valuable skill, can be a "black hole". If you play strictly from licks, especially if your lickabulary is limited, all of your solos may sound alike. On the other hand, if you develop a large lickabulary but apply it indiscriminately, your solos will be in poor taste. You have probably heard players whose every solo sounds like a banjo contest — too much flash and not enough melody. That is why we learned how to render a melody before we learned to improvise with licks.

Most banjoists learn songs by rote, and their arrangements are "carved in stone" — they are performed exactly the same every time. Even the best banjoists play mostly "patented" arrangements when performing. But for inexperienced players, even one missed note can lead to a "wreck" which cannot be recovered from without breaking time. When playing by rote, each note is linked to the adjacent one. When a note is missed, it is like breaking a link in a chain — the whole thing becomes nonfunctional. One important aspect of learning to view licks as interchangeable components is the enhanced ability to recover from mistakes without breaking time. When in trouble, experienced ear players can insert a familiar lick that fits the chord and allows him to return to the intended arrangement without timing lapse.

The accomplished player will play according to the guidelines of the situation. If playing in a band, where the main idea is to support the vocals, the ability to reproduce the melody and play tasteful backup is essential. The band members will be featured on an occasional instrumental number, in which they can show off their hot licks. In a jam session, the idea is to have fun — the rules are less strict. The general tone of the jam session can vary from mostly vocal backup with one or two solos per song, to all-out instrumental warfare. Most jam sessions fluctuate from one extreme to the other. If you are preparing for a contest or arranging a solo to be used in a band situation, melody playing and hot licks both go into producing an acceptable arrangement.

Expanding Your Lickabulary

The licks catalogued in this chapter are accepted elements of three-finger banjo style. As mentioned, you probably know many of them already, but may not view them as building blocks. Almost all of them are based on rolls. Listed below are the most popular roll patterns that can be combined with left-hand formations and slurs to form licks.

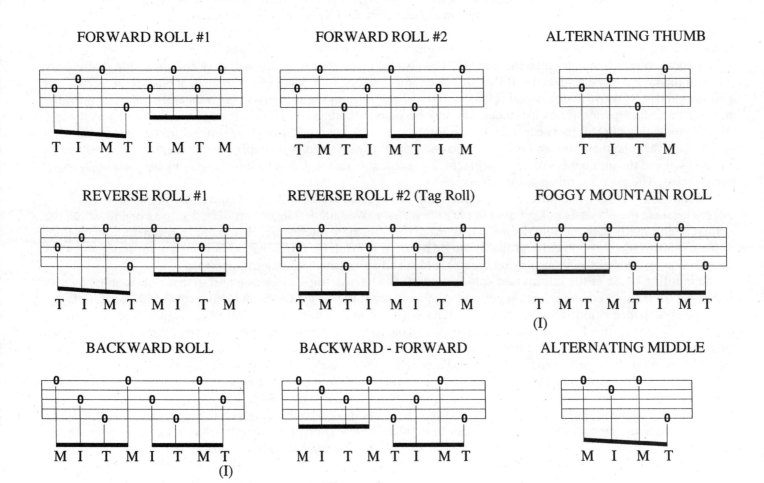

The licks catalogued in the following pages will include many slurs. Many of the licks will simply be ornamented versions of the faking patterns you learned in Chapter 2. Some may be totally new to you. All are in the accepted pool of banjo phrases. The licks labeled *a, b, c, etc.* can be played independently or combined to form longer licks.

G LICKS

Among these licks can be found the solution to most G chord melody situations. Most of the notes on the inside strings can be played on another string to access a particular melody note when necessary.

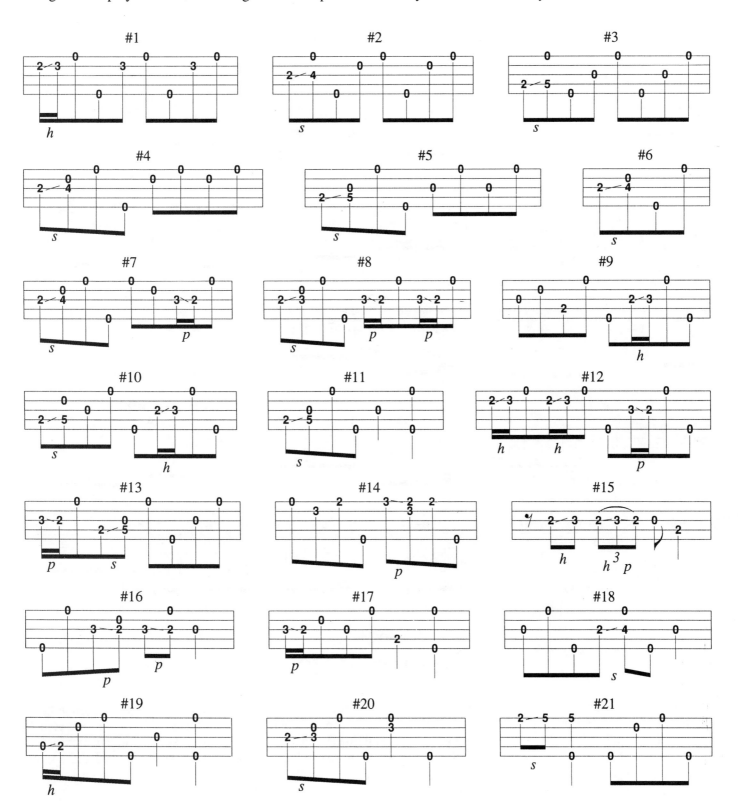

81

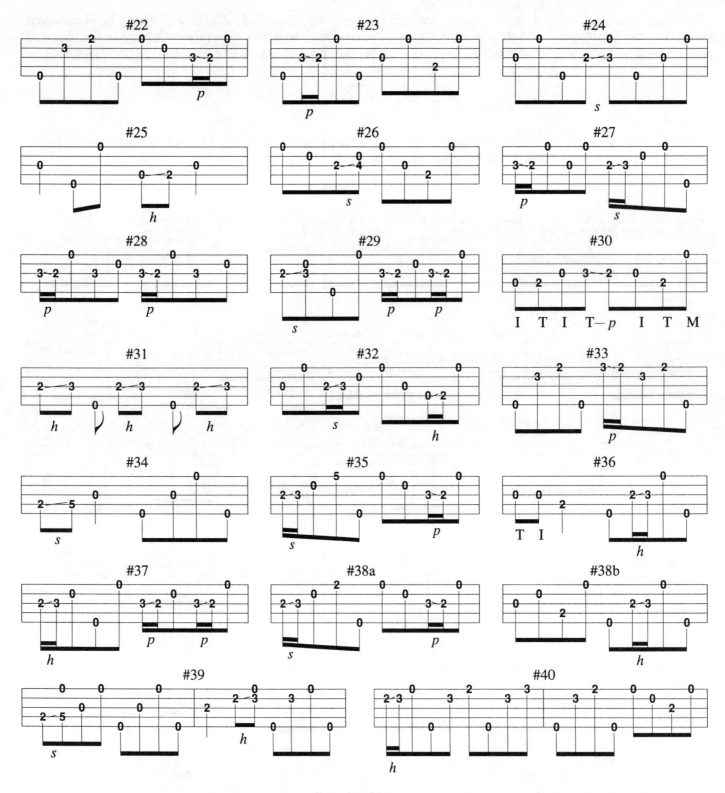

Exercise 22

INSERTING G LICKS

Memorize selected G licks from the preceding list. Return to the arrangements that you created for the song examples in this book and insert the chosen G licks in the appropriate places. When you find a location for a lick that sounds particularly appealing, play the altered arrangement several times to incorporate the new lick. Take time to experiment — do not assign a lick a permanent place in the song until you have tried several possibilities and found one that sounds particularly appealing to you. You may use the blank tablature found at the end of this chapter. Additional manuscript paper can be purchased at most music dealers.

C LICKS

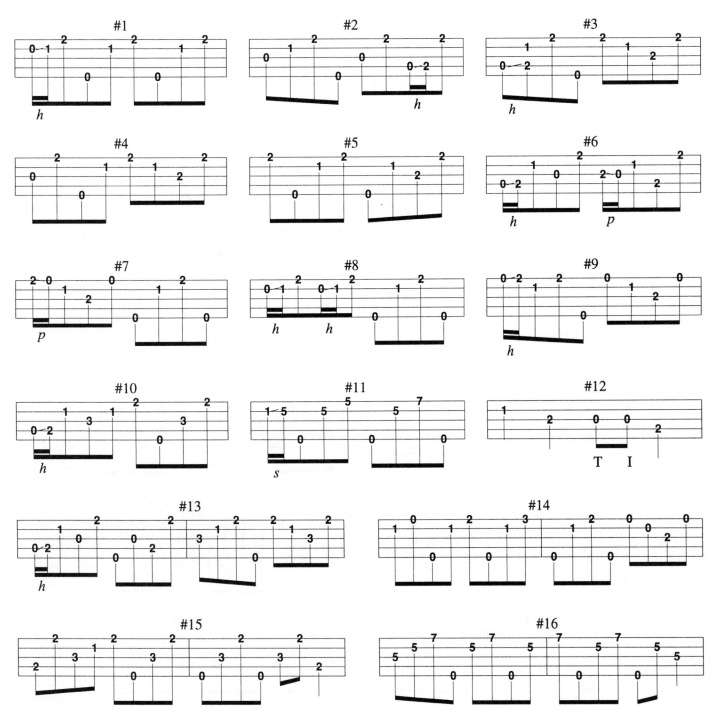

Exercise 23

INSERTING C LICKS

Memorize selected C licks from the preceding list. Return to the arrangements that you created for the song examples in this book and insert the chosen C licks in the appropriate places. When you find a location for a lick that sounds particularly appealing, play the altered arrangement several times to incorporate the new lick. Take time to experiment — do not assign a lick a permanent place in the song until you have tried several possibilities and found one that sounds particularly appealing to you. You may use the blank tablature found at the end of this chapter. Additional manuscript paper can be purchased at most music dealers.

D (or D7) LICKS

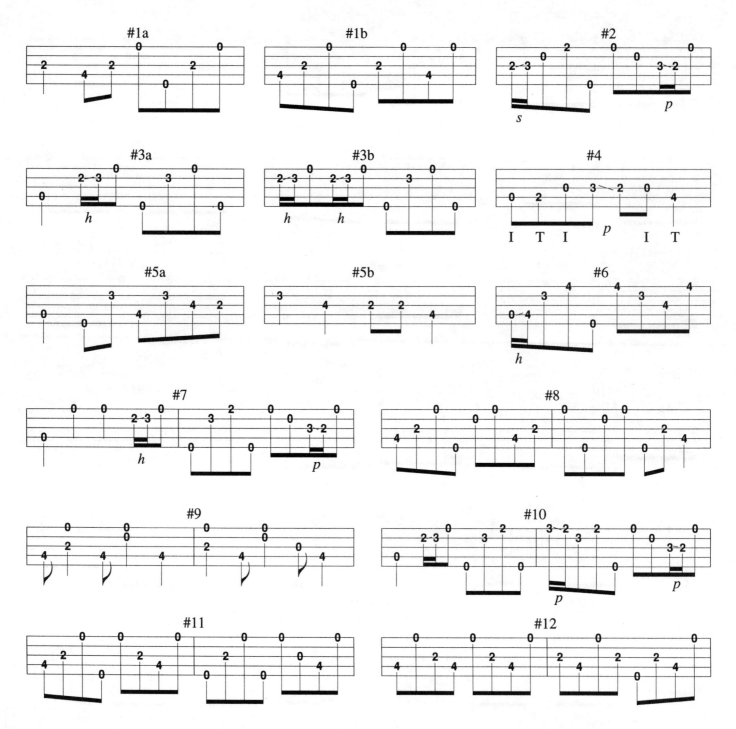

Exercise 24

INSERTING D (or D7) CHORD LICKS

Memorize selected D (or D7) licks from the preceding list. Return to the arrangements that you created for the song examples in this book and insert the chosen D (or D7) licks in appropriate places. When you find a location for a lick that sounds particularly appealing, play the altered arrangement several times to incorporate the new lick. Take time to experiment — do not assign a lick a permanent place in the song until you have tried several possibilities. You may use the blank tablature found at the end of this chapter. Additional manuscript paper can be purchased at most music dealers.

TAG LICK VARIATIONS

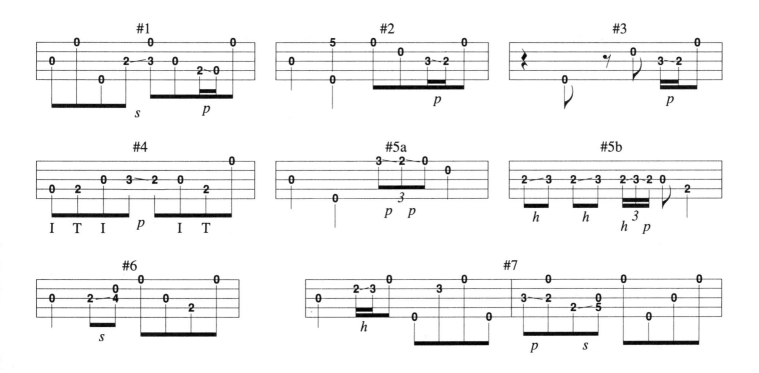

Exercise 25

INSERTING TAG LICK VARIATIONS

Memorize selected tag licks from the preceding list. Return to the arrangements that you created for the song examples in this book and insert the chosen tag licks in appropriate places. When you find a location for a lick that sounds particularly appealing, play the altered arrangement several times to incorporate the new lick. Take time to experiment — do not assign a lick a permanent place in the song until you have tried several possibilities and found one that sounds particularly appealing to you. You may use the blank tablature found below and at the end of this chapter. Additional manuscript paper can be purchased at most music dealers.

Altering Licks for Playability

Sometimes it will be necessary to alter a lick slightly in order to combine it smoothly with another. For example, since the Foggy Mountain roll ends with the thumb, you will not have time to begin the following roll with the thumb. Therefore, when a lick is chosen that involves the Foggy Mountain roll, some modification may be necessary. Shown below is a lick using the Foggy Mountain roll followed by a tag lick. The tag lick normally starts with the thumb. In order to avoid the repetition of the thumb after an eighth note, you will either have to *a)* replace the last note of the Foggy Mountain roll with a note that can be played with the index finger, *b)* omit the last note of the Foggy Mountain roll, or *c)* start the tag lick with the index finger.

FOGGY MOUNTAIN LICK + TAG LICK COMBINATION

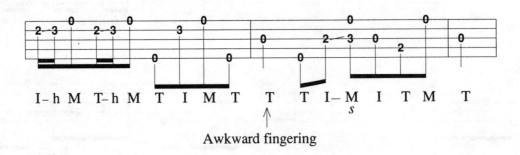

MODIFIED - LAST NOTE CHANGED

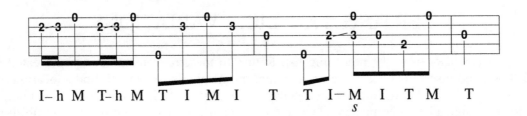

MODIFIED - LAST NOTE OMITTED

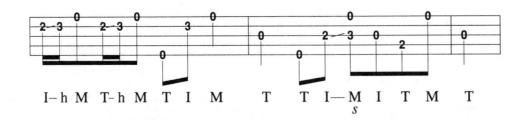

MODIFIED - INDEX ON FIRST NOTE OF TAG LICK

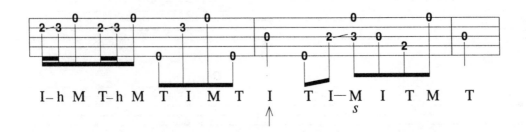

Faking with Licks

You used the patterns in Chapter 2 to fake entire solos based only on the chord progression. You can use the licks presented in this chapter to do likewise. Simply insert an appropriate lick into a given chord situation. Be sure to use phrasing licks in the appropriate places or the solo may not make sense compositionally. A faked solo for *Worried Man Blues* is shown below using licks selected from the lists in this chapter. The licks are labeled. Note that the solo bears no resemblance to the melody, though it would function as a "hot lick" solo late in the performance, after the melody has been well established.

Worried Man Blues - Faked Solo Using Licks

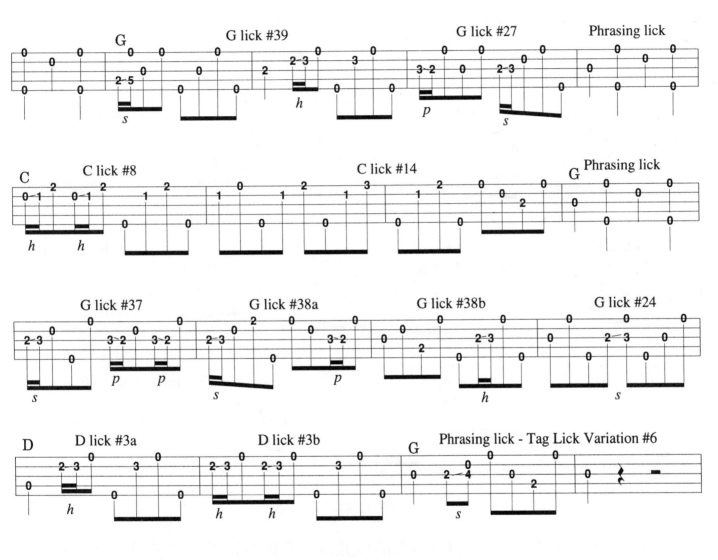

Exercise 26

USING LICKS TO FAKE SOLOS BY EAR

Refer to the sample chord progressions in Chapter 1. Construct faked solos for these progressions by inserting any of the appropriate licks into the chord progression. If you wish to record your arrangements, you may use the blank tablature at the end of this chapter and at various other places in this book. Additional manuscript paper can be purchased at most music dealers. Since the possibilities are virtually limitless, there will be no sample answer.

Creating a Melody Oriented Solo Using Licks

As mentioned, many of the licks catalogued here are merely fancier versions of the faking licks presented in Chapter 2. Almost all of them allow access to the inside strings on the all-important first and last beats of the measure. You can select licks that allow you to render any of the melodies you learned by ear in Chapter 3, or any other vocal melody you may encounter. *Worried Man Blues* is arranged below using licks selected from the lists in this chapter to render an accurate melody.

Worried Man Blues - Melody Oriented Solo Using Licks

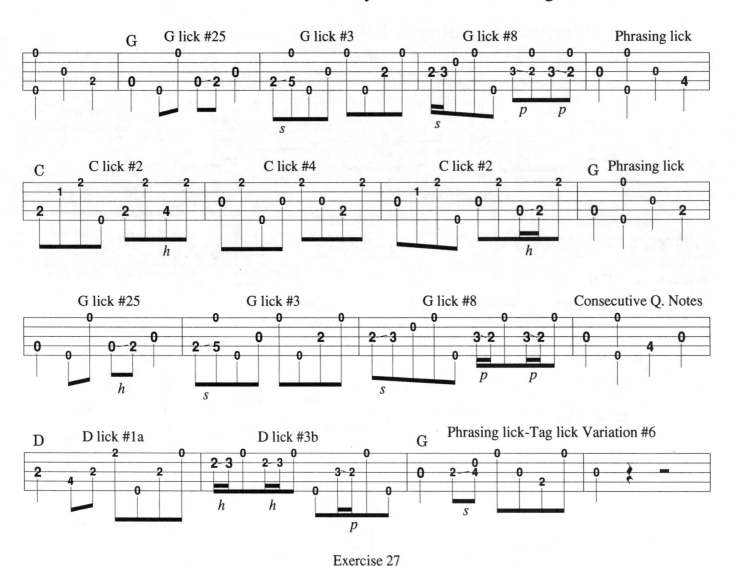

Exercise 27

USING LICKS TO CREATE A MELODY ORIENTED SOLO BY EAR

Return to the arrangements that you created for the song examples in this book. From the previous lists, select licks that will best allow access to the proper melody notes. Remember, it is not necessary to sound every melody note, though you should try to sound at least the first melody note of each measure or phrase. Remember also that a melody note can be shifted forward or backward a half beat to accommodate a roll pattern. To avoid awkward right-hand finger sequences and to facilitate faster position changing, you may omit eighth notes to create quarter notes. If you wish to record your arrangement, you may use the blank tablature at the end of this chapter and at various other places in this book. Additional manuscript paper can be purchased at most music dealers. Since the possibilities are virtually limitless, there will be no sample answer.

Adapting Licks

Though most of these licks are based on a particular chord, you may alter many of them for use with other chords. Simply hold the desired chord formation and play the same or a slightly altered right-hand pattern. For example:

The first G lick on page 81 can be adapted for use in an A chord situation:

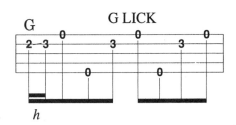
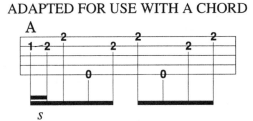

The first C lick on page 83 can be adapted for use in an E chord situation:

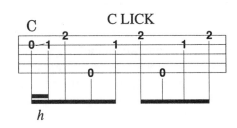
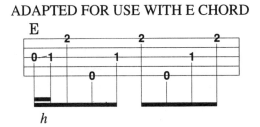

The first D lick on page 84 can be adapted for use in an F chord situation:

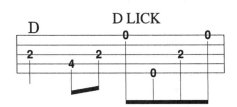
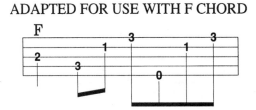

The basic G tag lick can be adapted for phrases that end in a C chord situation:

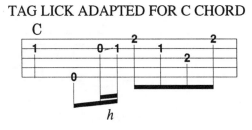

Exercise 28

ADAPTING LICKS

Adapt selected G, C, and D (or D7) licks to create lick-based solos for Song Examples #7 - #12. You may use the blank tablature in the back of this book to record your arrangements. Additional manuscript paper can be purchased at most music dealers. Since the possibilities are virtually limitless, there will be no sample answer presented.

Style

Some licks may not sound esthetically pleasing when combined. They may be totally different melodically, or too much the same. Certain licks may contain too much dissonance to be used adjacently, or a lick may not render a melody accurately enough to be acceptable to you. These are subjective decisions, and will take thoughtful experimentation to work out. This is part of the fun and the challenge in becoming an accomplished player. This is also how your personal style evolves. As you worked through the exercises in this book you selected favorite licks and certain ways to combine these licks. It is the things you choose to incorporate, the things you choose to leave out, and your level of execution that make your playing unique.

Musicians are like snowflakes — there are no two alike. Even two banjoists who play the same arrangements at the same tempo on the same banjo will sound different. This difference is what style is all about. The more you experiment and practice, the more your personal style will emerge. The diligent application of the concepts presented will result in much more than the ability to play by ear — it will result in your developing a style that is uniquely your own.

Beyond Licks

After much experience using licks to compose arrangements, it will be possible to create arrangements "on the fly" simply by thinking of a melody. The licks will become so internalized that for any given melody situation, a lick will simply "happen" as you play. Reaching this level is simply a result of working with these concepts so much that the whole process becomes subconscious. The only way to get there is through experience. All this book can do is explain the process. The progress in learning to teach yourself by ear takes place as a result of hundreds of hours of practice. So get busy!

Use the blank tablature that follows for notes or to create arrangements.

APPENDIX

ANSWERS TO EXERCISES

Exercise 1, Page 8

DETERMINING METER

1 4/4	4 4/4	7 4/4	10 4/4
2 4/4	5 4/4	8 4/4	11 4/4
3 3/4	6 3/4	9 4/4	12 4/4

Exercise 2, Pages 9–10

HEARING SIMPLE CHORD CHANGES

Progression #1:
Meter:____4/4____

Verse/Chorus:

x   x

x   x   x   x   x

Progression #2:
Meter:____4/4____

Verse:

x   x   x

x   x

Chorus:

x   x   x   x   x

x   x   x

Progression #3:
Meter:____3/4____

Verse/Chorus:

x   x   x   x

x   x   x   x   x

HEARING CHORD CHANGES WITHIN THE MEASURE

Progression #4:
Meter: 4/4

Verse:

X												X	X										X	X

Chorus:

											X	X										X	X

Progression #5:
Meter: 4/4

Verse:

X				X	X				X	X				X	X		X	X

Chorus:

											X	X										X	X

Progression #6:
Meter: 3/4

Verse/Chorus:

X		X	X					X	X			X			X	

X			X				X	X				X	X	

LEARNING "BASIC THREE" PROGRESSIONS BY EAR

Progression #1:
Meter: 4/4

Verse/Chorus:

G						D	

G		C		G	D	G	

Progression #2:
Meter: 4/4

Verse/Chorus:

G				D		G	

G				D		G	

Chorus:

C		G		C		G	D

G				D		G	

Progression #3:
Meter: 3/4

Verse/Chorus:

G		C	G			D	

G		C	G		D	G	

Progression #4:
Meter: 4/4

Verse:

G			D	G			D G

Chorus:

			D G				D G

Progression #5:
Meter: 4/4

Verse:

G		C	G	D	G		C	G	D G

Chorus:

			D G				D G

Progression #6:
Meter: 3/4

Verse/Chorus:

G C	G		D	G	D	G

D	G		C	G		D	G

LEARNING PROGRESSIONS CONTAINING ONE SUPPORTING CHORD

Progression #7:
Meter:____4/4____

Verse/Chorus:

G		F		G	D	G	

G		F		G	D	G	

Progression #8:
Meter:____4/4____

Verse/Chorus:

G				C		G	

C		G	Em	G	D	G	

Progression #9:
Meter:____4/4____

Verse:

G		C	G	C	G	A	D

G		C	G	C	G	D	G

Chorus:

C		G		D		G	

C		G		D		G	

LEARNING PROGRESSIONS CONTAINING TWO SUPPORTING CHORDS

Progression #10:
Meter:____4/4____

Verse/Chorus:

C		G		C		G	

	B7	C		G	D	G	

Progression #11:
Meter: ___4/4___

Verse/Chorus:

G	E	A		D		G	

G	E	A		D		G	

Progression #12:
Meter: ___4/4___

Verse/Chorus:

G						D	

					D7	G	

G					G7	C	

	C#°	G	E7	A7	D7	G	

Exercise 7, Page 24

IDENTIFYING MAJOR, MINOR AND SEVENTH CHORD TYPES

1	B		21	B
2	C		22	A
3	A		23	B
4	C		24	C
5	B		25	C
6	A		26	A
7	B		27	B
8	A		28	A
9	C		29	C
10	A		30	A
11	B		31	B
12	C		32	B
13	B		33	C
14	B		34	A
15	A		35	C
16	C		36	B
17	B		37	A
18	A		38	B
19	C		39	C
20	A		40	A

FAKING SOLOS BASED ON "BASIC THREE" PROGRESSIONS
Progression #1

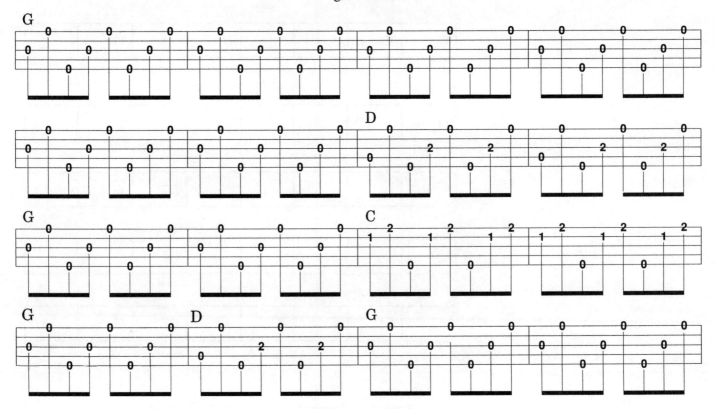

USING PHRASING LICKS
Progression #1

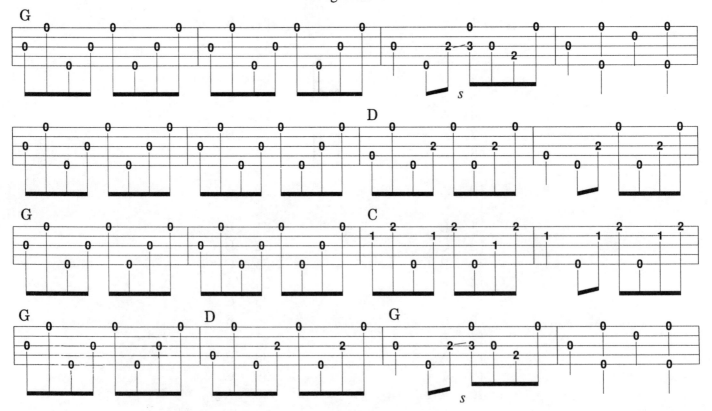

Progression #2

Verse:

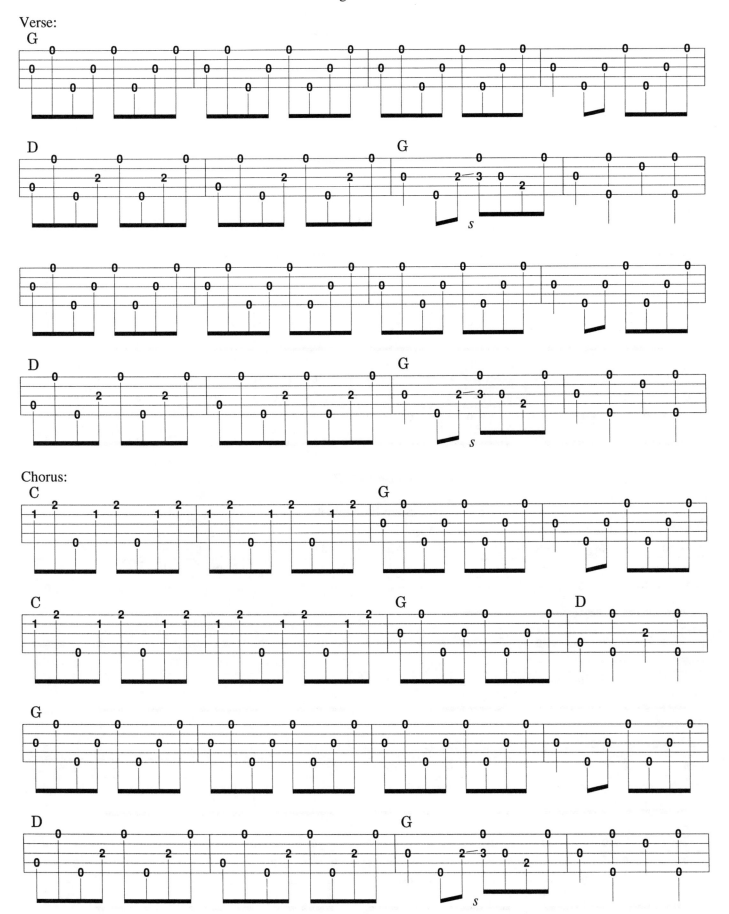

Chorus:

FAKING A SOLO BASED ON A QUICKLY CHANGING PROGRESSION
Sample Answer

Song Example #4

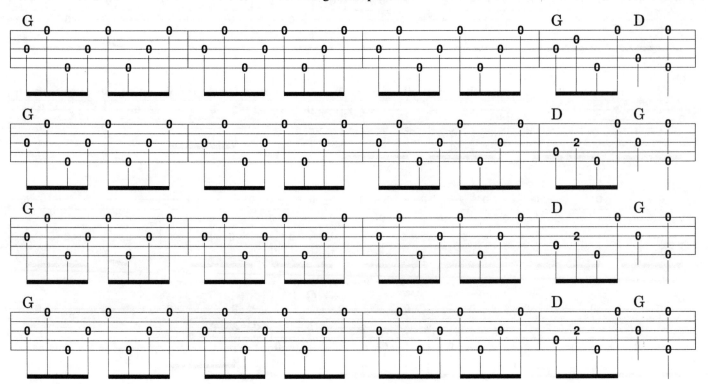

Exercise 10 b, Page 34

Song Example #5

Verse:

Chorus:

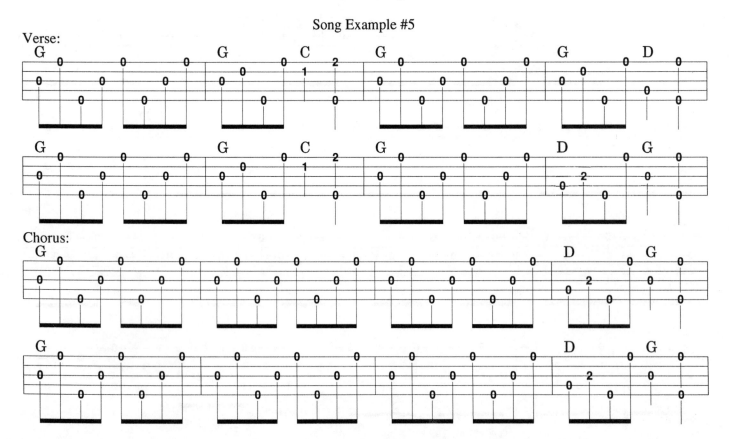

FAKING SOLOS BASED ON 3/4 TIME PROGRESSIONS

Song Example #3 - Faked Solo

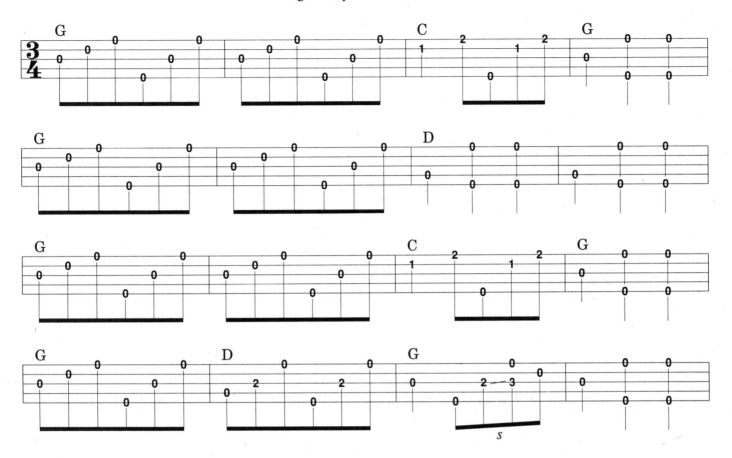

Sample Song #6 - Faked Solo

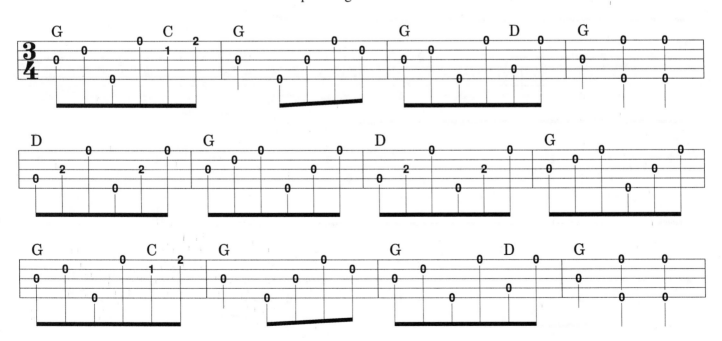

FAKING SOLOS BASED ON COMPLEX PROGRESSIONS

Exercise 12 a - Progression #7, Page 39:

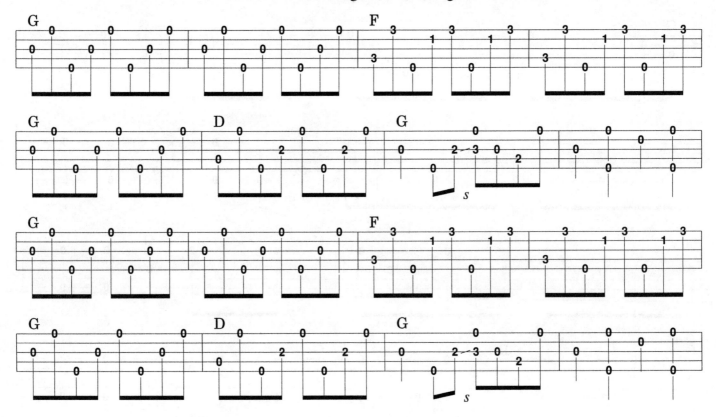

Exercise 12 b - Progression #8, Page 39:

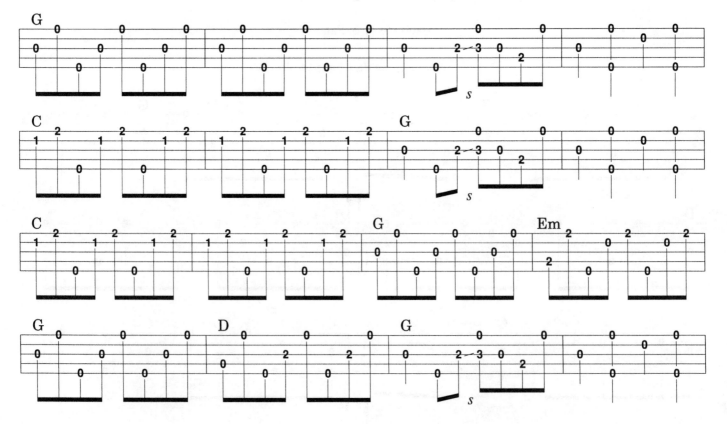

Exercise 12 c - Progression #9, Page 40:

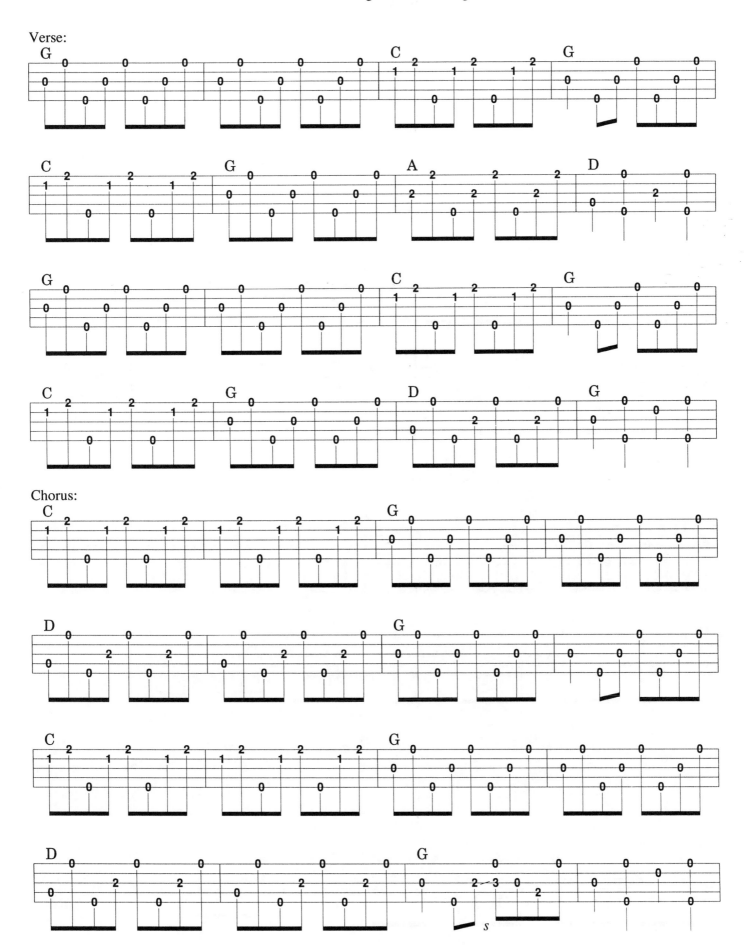

Exercise 12 d - Progression #10, Page 41:

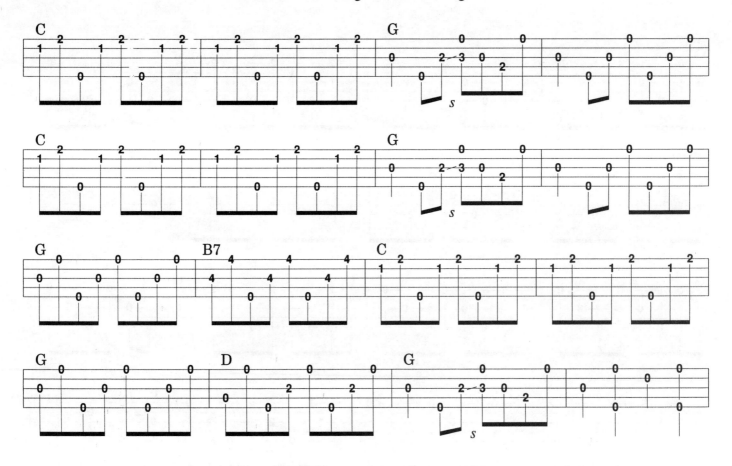

Exercise 12 e - Progression #11, Page 41:

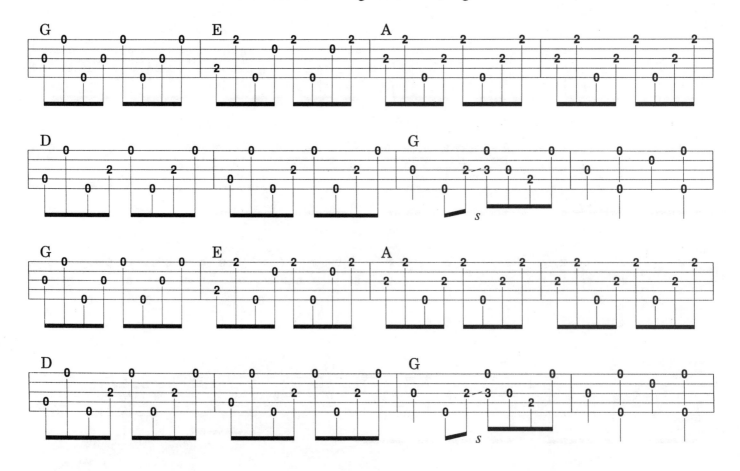

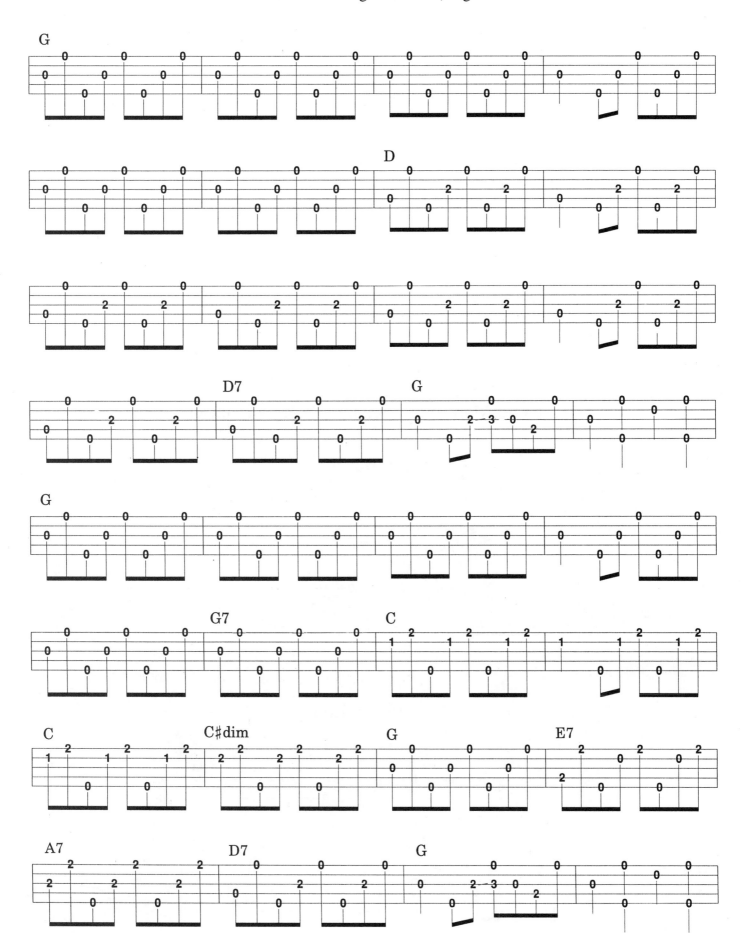

IDENTIFYING SIMPLE MELODY LINES

Mary Had a Little Lamb

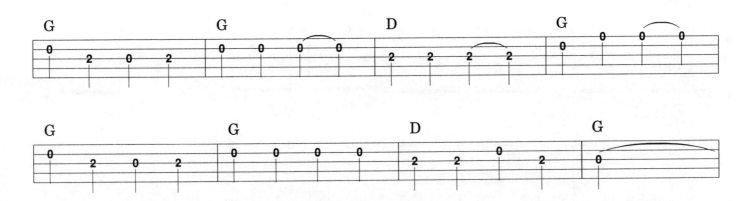

This Old Man (Nick- Knack, Paddy- Whack)

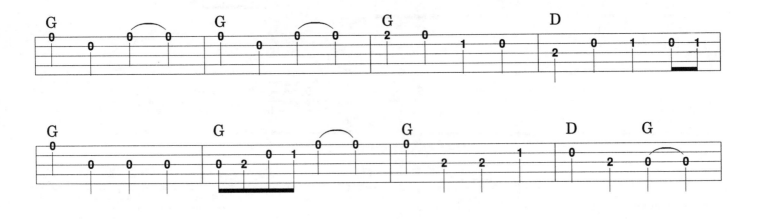

Skip to My Lou

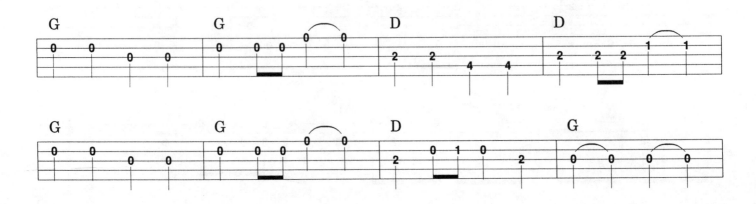

ALTERING A FAKED SOLO TO CREATE A MELODY ORIENTED SOLO

Song Example #1 - First-beat Melody Notes

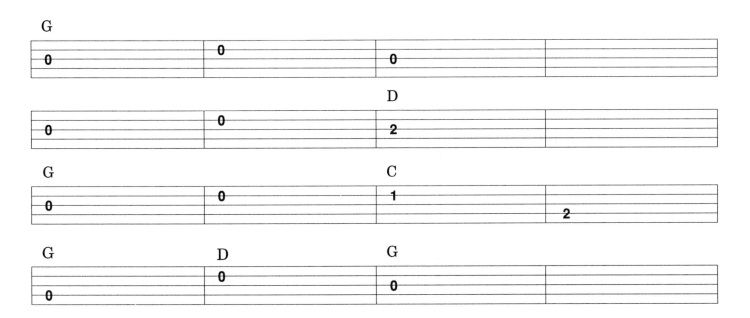

Exercise 15, Page 58

Song Example #1- Faked Solo, Altered to Create a Melody Oriented Solo
(Sample answer- there is no one correct answer.)

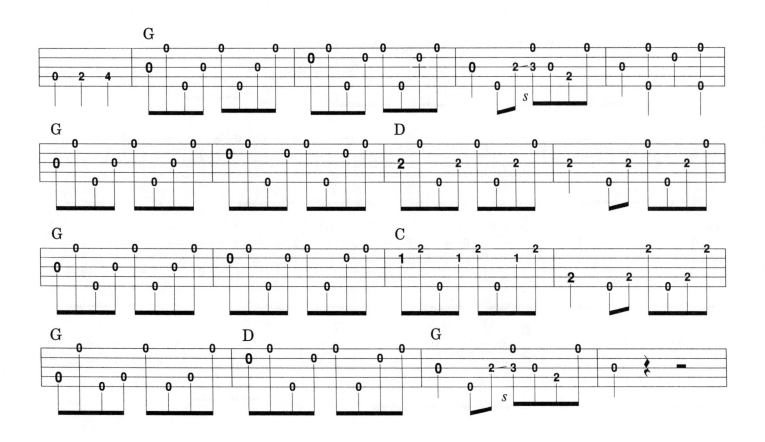

CREATING A FIRST-BEAT AND LAST-BEAT MELODY ARRANGEMENT

Song Example #1 - First-beat and Last-beat Melody Notes

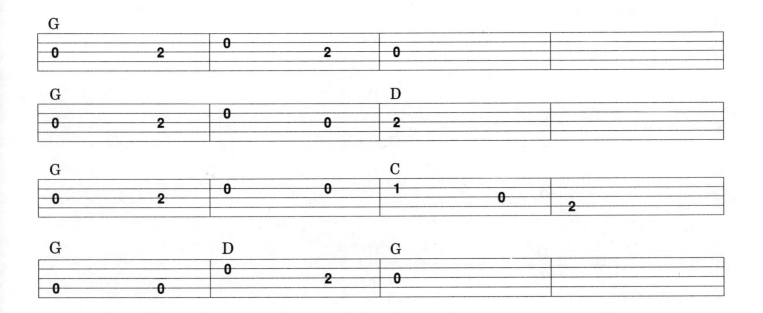

Song Example #1 - First-beat and Last-beat Melody Oriented Solo

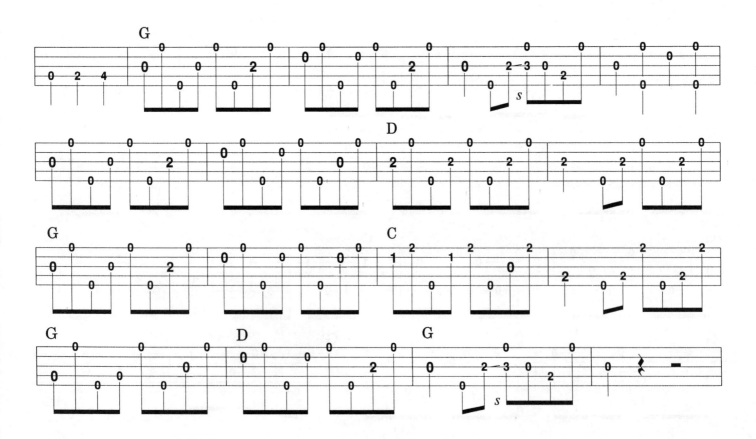

Exercise 16 b, Page 62

Song Example #2 - First-beat and Last-beat Melody Notes

Verse:

```
      G
|-----------------|---------------------|------------------|
|-----------1--3--|---------------------|-----------0------|
|--2---0----------|---------------------|------------------|
|-----------------|---------------------|------------------|
```

```
  D                               G
|-3--------3------|-----------------------------|------------------|
|------------2----2--0------------------------|------------------2-|
|-----------------|-----------------------------|------------------|
```

```
  G
|-----------------|---------------------|------------------|
|-----------1--3--|---------------------|-----------0------|
|-0---------------|---------------------|------------------|
```

```
  D                               G                              0
|-3--------3------|-----------------------------|------------------|
|------------2----2--0------------------------|------------------|
|-----------------|-----------------------------|------------------|
```

Chorus:

```
  C                               G
|-5--------5------5--3--------3--0-----|
|------------5----------------------------|
|-----------------|------------------------|
```

```
  C                               G        D
|-5--------5------5--3---------------|
|------------5--------------2--------2-|
|-----------------|-----------------------|
```

```
  G
|-----------------|---------------------|------------------|
|-----------1--3--|---------------------|-----------0------|
|-0---------------|---------------------|------------------|
```

```
  D                               G
|-3--------3------|-----------------------------|------------------|
|------------2----2--0------------------------|------------------|
|-----------------|-----------------------------|------------------|
```

Song Example #2 - First-beat and Last-beat Melody Oriented Solo

Verse:

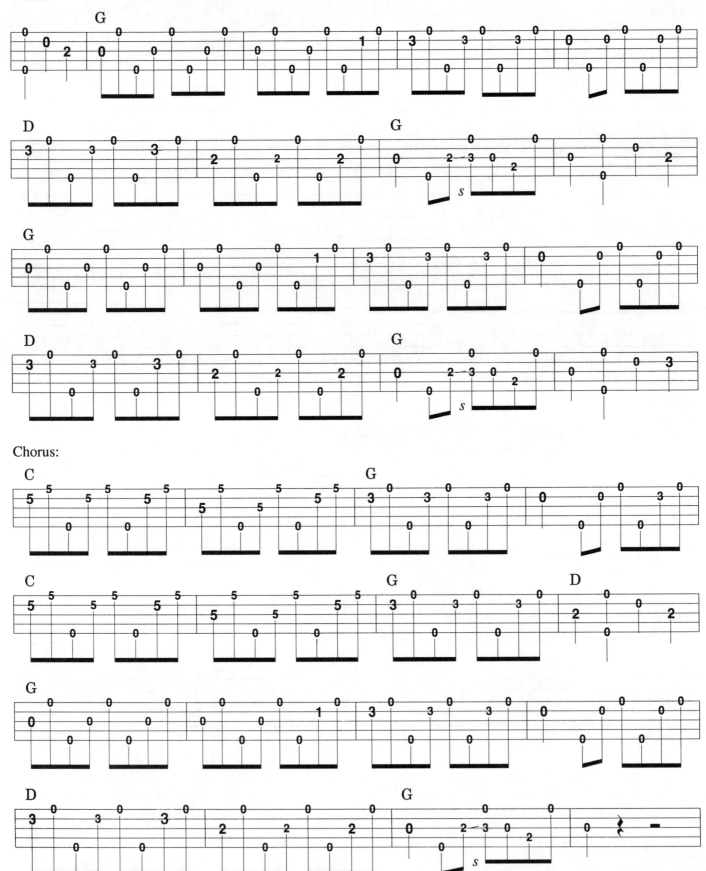

Chorus:

CREATING A SOLO INCLUDING ALL ACCESSIBLE MELODY NOTES

Song Example #1- All Melody Notes

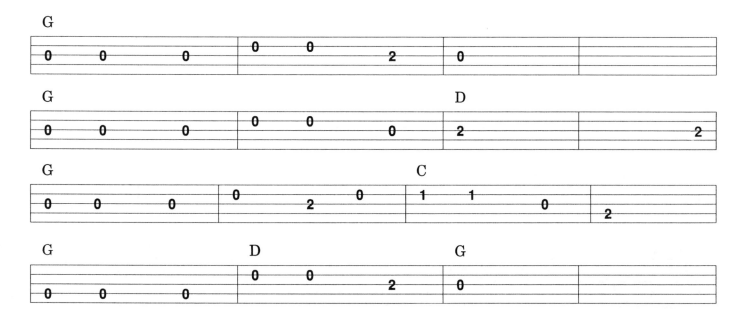

Song Example #1- Melody Oriented Solo with All Accessible Melody Notes

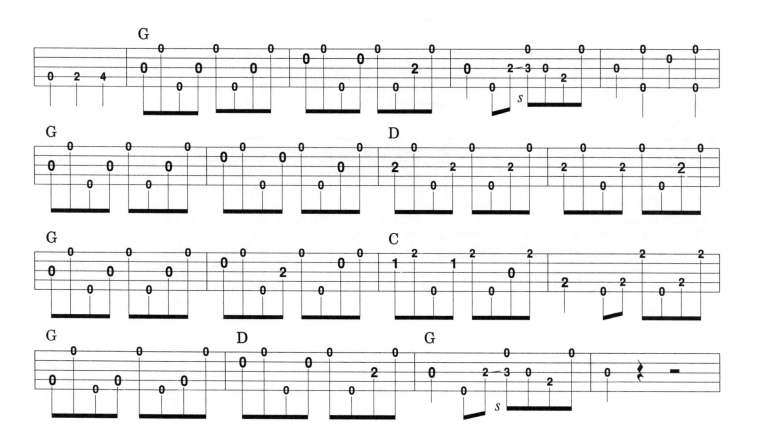

Song Example #2 - All Melody Notes

Verse:

```
         G
|-0-----|---------|-----0---1-|-3-------|-----0-----|
|---2-0-|-------0-|-----------|---------|-----------|
```

```
 D                           G
|-3-------3-|-------------0-----|-0-------|-----0---|
|-----------2---2-----2-----|-----------|-------2-|
```

```
 G
|-0-------|-------0---0---1-|-3-------|-----0-----|
```

```
 D                           G
|-3-------3-|-------------0-----|-0-------|-----0-----0|
|-----------2---2-----2-----|-----------|-----------|
```

Chorus:

```
 C                               G
|-5-------5-|-------------5-|-3-------|-----0-----0-----0|
|-----------5---5---7-------|---------|-----------|
```

```
 C                               G                 D
|-5-------5-|-------------5-|-3-------0-|-------0-----|
|-----------5---5---7-------|-----------|---2-------2-|
```

```
 G
|-0-------|-------0---0---1-|-3-------|-----0-----|
```

```
 D                           G
|-3-------3-|-------0-----|-0-------|
|-----------2---2-----2-----|---------|
```

Song Example #2- Melody Oriented Solo with All Accessible Melody Notes

Verse:

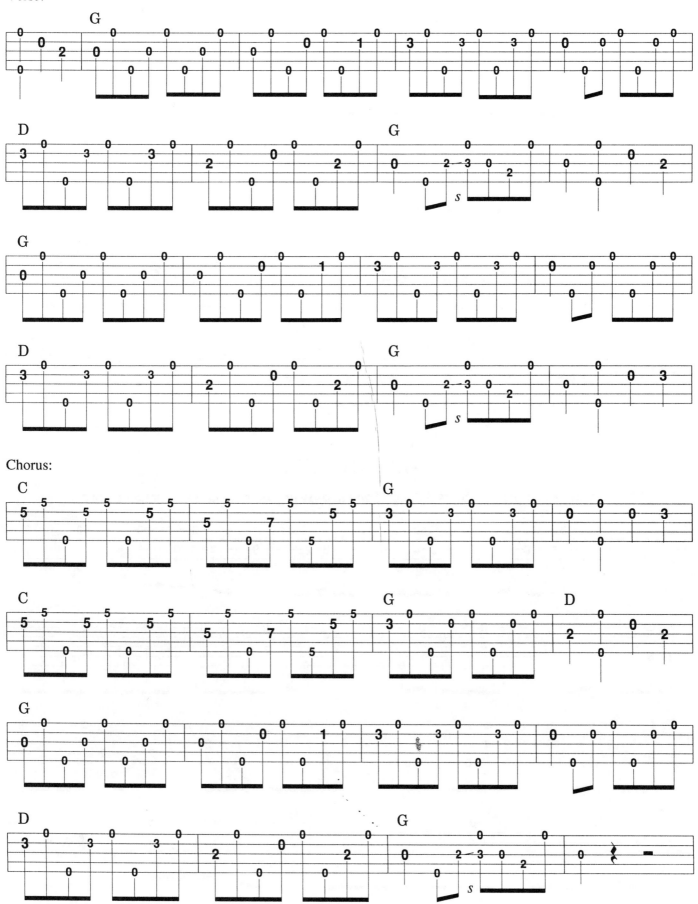

Chorus:

Exercise 18, Page 70
USING QUARTER NOTES

Song Example #1 - Quarter Notes Added *(Sample answer - there is no one correct answer)*

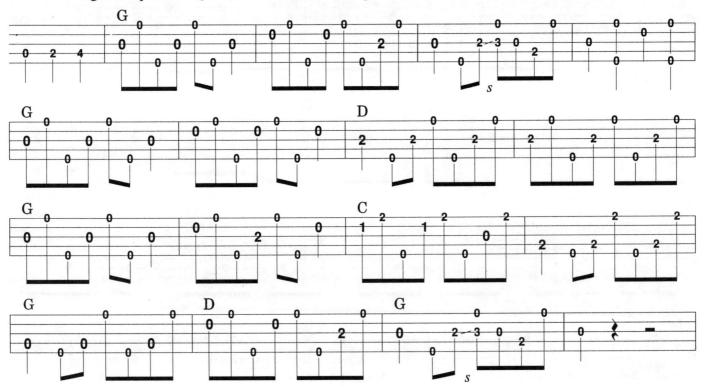

Exercise 19, Page 72
ADDING SLURS

Song Example #1 - Slurs Added *(Sample answer - there is no one correct answer)*

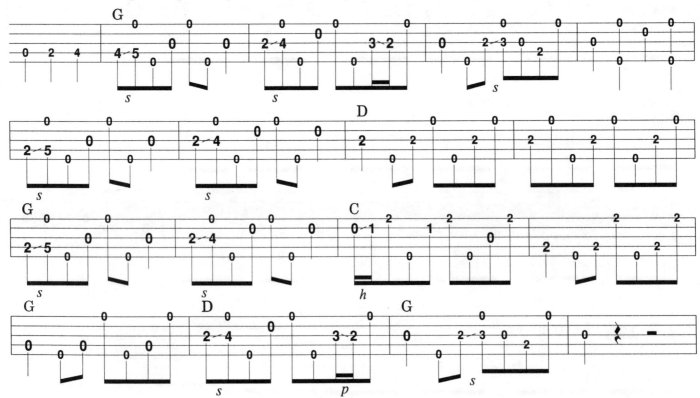

CREATING QUICKLY CHANGING MELODY SOLOS BY EAR

Song Example #4 - Melody

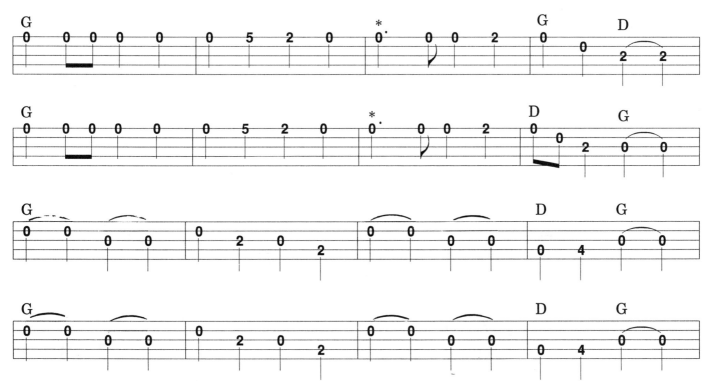

* A dot after a note adds half again value to it. A dotted quarter note lasts one and a half beats.

Song Example #4 - Melody Oriented Solo

(Sample answer - there is no one correct answer)

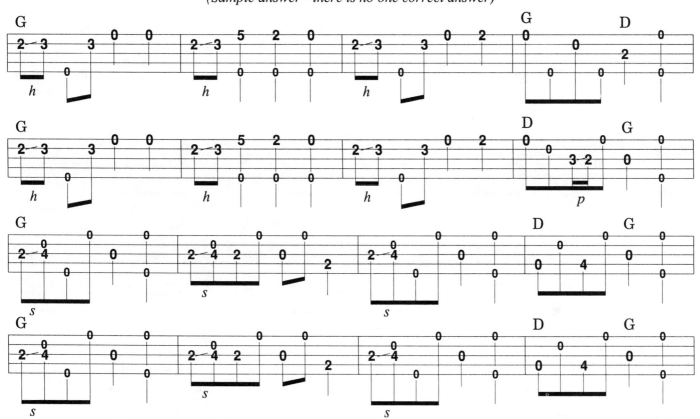

Song Example #5 - Melody

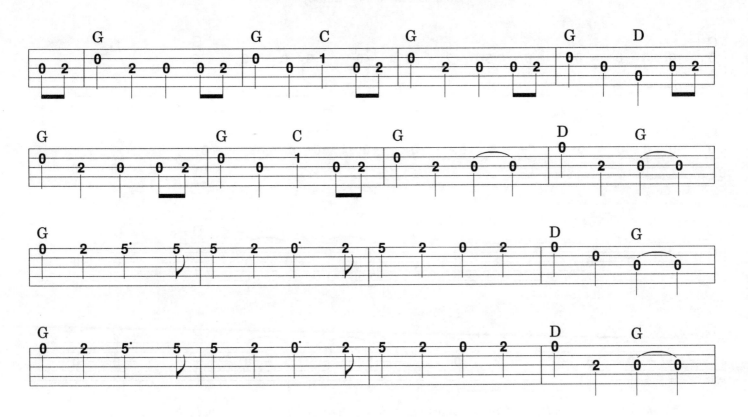

Song Example #5 - Melody Oriented Solo
(Sample — there is no one correct answer)

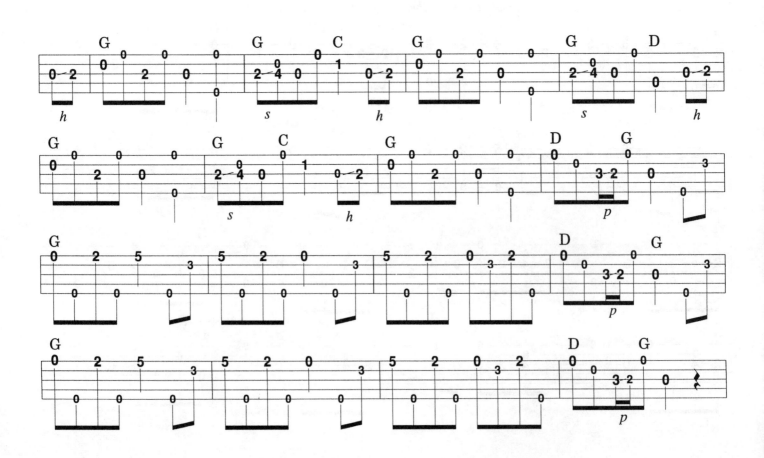

CREATING A MELODY ORIENTED SOLO IN 3/4 TIME

Song Example #3 - Melody

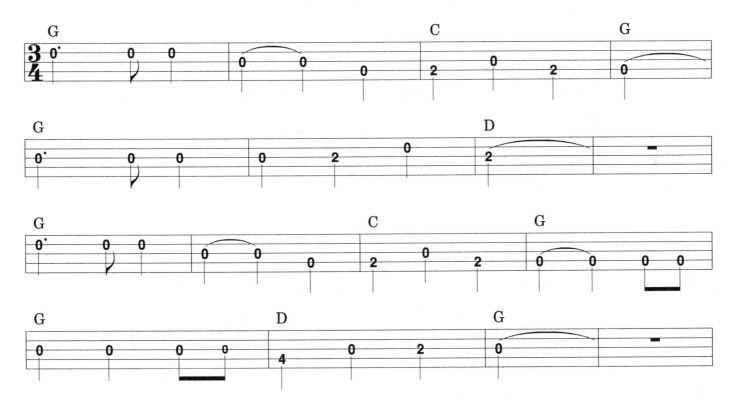

Song Example #3 - Melody Oriented Solo

(Sample - there is no one correct answer)

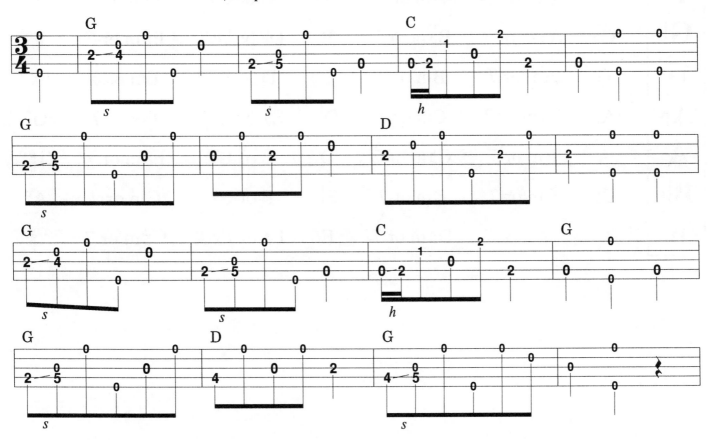

TRANSPOSITION CHART

The explanations in this book are in the key of G major, which is the most popular key for bluegrass banjo players. The transposition chart below will help you apply the information to any of the twelve major keys.

FREQUENTLY USED DIATONIC TRIADS
AND DOMINANT SEVENTH CHORDS IN ALL TWELVE KEYS

NUMBER NAME	1	2m or 7	3m or 7	4	5 or 57	6m or 7	7°
KEY				LETTER NAME			
C	C	Dm or 7	Em or 7	F	G or G7	Am or 7	B°
D♭	D♭	E♭m or 7	Fm or 7	G♭	A♭ or A♭7	B♭m or 7	C°
D	D	Em or 7	F♯m or 7	G	A or A7	Bm or 7	C♯°
E♭	E♭	Fm or 7	Gm or 7	A♭	B♭ or B♭7	Cm or 7	D°
E	E	F♯m or 7	G♯m or 7	A	B or B7	C♯m or 7	D♯°
F	F	Gm or 7	Am or 7	B♭	C or C7	Dm or 7	E°
G♭	G♭	A♭m or 7	B♭m or 7	B	D♭ or D♭7	E♭m or 7	F°
G	G	Am or 7	Bm or 7	C	D or D7	Em or 7	F♯°
A♭	A♭	B♭m or 7	Cm or 7	D♭	E♭ or E♭7	Fm or 7	G°
A	A	Bm or 7	C♯m or 7	D	E or E7	F♯m or 7	G♯°
B♭	B♭	Cm or 7	Dm or 7	E♭	F or F7	Gm or 7	A°
B	B	C♯m or 7	D♯m or 7	E	F♯ or F♯7	G♯m or 7	A♯°